DARE

to be a

Man of God

Powerful Bible studies for young men
today on listening to God's voice
and winning life's battles

Mikaela Vincent

Text and illustrations copyright © 2016 by Mikaela Vincent

More Than A Conqueror Books

MoreThanAConquerorBooks@gmail.com
www.MoreThanAConquerorBooks.com

MANY MEN OF GOD have covered me throughout the writing of this Bible study/devotional. I'm especially grateful to my husband and son for their contributions and to my Godly mentors and friends who helped with content and editing.

As the wife of a true man of God, I originally wrote this book to equip our son with powerful tools and weapons of truth for the battles he would face in life. As he has grown into a man of God now and many more spiritual sons have joined the ranks of studying these truths, the Lord led me to re-release this book for every single man who wishes to listen to God's voice, walk in the Spirit and overcome the enemy.

If you have any questions, please write
MoreThanAConquerorBooks@gmail.com

or message Mikaela Vincent on **Facebook** at
https://www.facebook.com/mikaela.vincent.author and/or
https://www.facebook.com/Mikaela.Vincent.MoreThanAConquerorBooks

You can also follow my blog at
MoreThanAConquerorBooks.wordpress.com
and find me on **Twitter** and **Instagram @Mikaela.Vincent**,
and on **Pinterest** at **Mikaela Vincent: More Than A Conqueror Books**

May He bless you richly as you become
the man of God He created you to be!

"*Dare to Be a Man of God* is a powerful book for a young man. It meets him where he needs encouragement, support, spiritual encouragement, empowering, and the wisdom to see how God is working in his life. The author uses Scripture wisely and effectively to draw a young man's attention to his powerful God. Every parent or person who loves a young man will have confidence knowing that this book will speak of truth to a male's needs."

— Kathryn Miller, author of *Never Ever Be the Same: A New You Starts Today*

Contents

To my spiritual sons, the young men who will read this book:

I originally wrote this workbook to study together with my son, because when I looked for a Bible study or devotional to equip him to truly become a powerful man of God, nothing I found on the shelves of Christian bookstores went deep enough.

*In order to triumph over the enemy in this world as it is, young men today must have the tools and models to live in **"the whole measure of the fullness of Christ."** Ephesians 4:13 (NIV) There is just too much at stake to settle for the Christian "norm."*

*Your marriage, children and all the broken lives around you need a radical man of God who lives in the power of the only One Who can change the world. **Will you dare to become that man of God?***

God wants to equip you to climb the steep faces of every mountain and rappel off every cliff in life with excitement and faith, not fear.

The Word of God is your lifeline.

So hold on tightly to the truth, wrap it around your waist (Ephesians 6:14), and secure it to your heart, until the truth you know becomes the truth you live.

*Don't be discouraged if some of the qualities of a man of God on these pages seem out of your reach, especially if you never grew up with a Godly example in your household. **You have a true and perfect Heavenly Father Who wants to show you how it's done.***

So keep climbing. He'll point out the secure footholds so you won't slip. And if you fall, He is able to catch you.

The mistakes that were made before you don't have to continue on down your family line. They can stop now with you, if you choose. You can be the one who makes the choice to live as God created you to be and enjoy life to its fullest in Him.

Most of all, love God with all your heart, and never doubt His fathomless love for you.

My hope is that you, like my amazing husband and son, will become a man of God (if you aren't one already!), and the woman you marry will be blessed beyond measure, just as I have been.

I dare you to be a Man of God!

"Momma" Mikaela

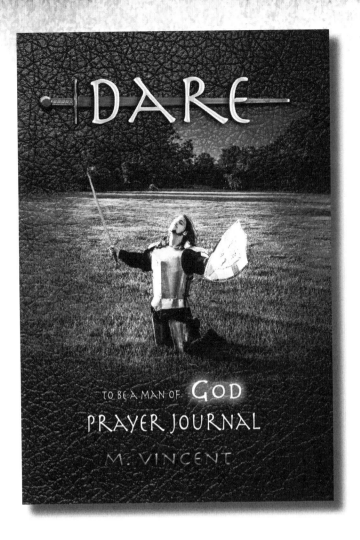

Complete the dare with

Dare to Be a Man of God Prayer Journal
by Mikaela Vincent

The power of God is just a quiet time away!

Packed with tools for drawing near to God, listening to His voice, and walking in the Spirit, this prayer journal is a companion to *Dare to Be a Man of God.*

Available with or without lines from
www.MoreThanAConquerorBooks.com.

Author's proceeds go to shining the light of Christ where it's never been before. For more information on the Vincents and their ministry, write

MoreThanAConquerorBooks@gmail.com.

How to use this workbook:

1. **Keep a journal.** You were created for relationship. So think of your journal as letters written by you to Someone you love, and from your Loved One to you. Let Him change the way you see things. And keep looking back at what He's teaching you so you won't forget it, and so you can walk out in those truths. *Let Him change your life.* A ***Dare to Be a Man of God Prayer Journal*** is available at www.MoreThanAConquerorBooks.com, both with lines and without (for those who may like to draw or do other creative journaling), as a perfect companion to this book. It's loaded with tools for winning the battle through prayer.

2. **Look up the scriptures in each chapter.** It's God's words that will change you, not mine. So don't skip looking up any of the references. I like to write in the margins of my Bible the things He is teaching me from each passage. Then every time I open my Bible to that passage I'm reminded of what He said, and it's easier to walk out in that truth.

3. **Take your time through each chapter.** Don't be in a hurry to get through this book. Every chapter has deep jewels in it God wants you to truly learn and walk out in, not just skim through. The daily applications at the end of each chapter are lifestyle-changing, if you let them become a habit rather than something you do just once. You might want to continue using this devotional even after you've completed it, going back through the daily applications so you can get in the habit of doing those things and asking your heart those questions again and again.

4. **Have a daily quiet time.** Don't let a day go by without time alone with Jesus. Everyone's quiet time is different, so don't feel like yours has to look like someone else's or happen at the same time of day as theirs. Feel free to be creative. I like to start my morning with Jesus, just doing whatever He's doing that day: worshipping, listening to Him, praying, reading the Word, letting Him show me things in my heart He wants to change, or studying through a devotional. Then at night, I read the Bible (I like to just read until He shows me something, and then stop, meditate on what He said, and pray it back to Him), so that what He says is the last thing in my mind as I fall asleep.

5. **Get your friends involved.** Introduce this devotional to others who will journey with you through it, doing the chapters in their own quiet times or in a group study, talking together with you each week about what God is showing them. You will learn more if you are sharing what you're learning, and hearing what He's teaching others. (See suggestions at the end of the book for how to lead a group Bible study.)

Warning:

The information on these pages
may change the course of your life.

Before you read any further,

Pray!

God, open my eyes to see what You want me to see...

To hear Your voice...

To know You more...

To walk in Your ways ...

To become like You...

Part 1

*"Where your treasure is, there your heart will be also.
... No one can serve two masters; for either he will
hate the one and love the other, or else he will be loyal
to the one and despise the other. ... But seek first the
kingdom of God and His righteousness, and all these
things shall be added to you."*

Matthew 6:21, 24, 33

First Things First

Chapter 1

~ to seek God's Kingdom first

What do you want most?

If a genie promised to grant you three wishes, what would you wish for?

1. _____
2. _____
3. _____

Would that really be enough to make you happy for the rest of your life?

The truth is, *no matter how hard you run after the things you want or need in life, they will never satisfy you.* **Only a deep, intimate relationship with Christ will.**

Why? *Because it's what you were created for.*

No one on this earth gets to live a problem-free life. But we *can* live a *joy*-filled life, if we tap into the right Source. John 10:10.

The key to contentment is found in Psalm 87:7: *"All my springs are in you."*

If you know Who the Source of your joy is you will never wander far, for your thirst will always drive you back to Him.

That's how Paul could say in Philippians 4:12-13 (NIV):

*"I know what it is to be in need, and I know what it is to have plenty. I have learned **the secret of being content** in any and every situation, whether well fed or hungry, whether living in plenty or in want. **I can do everything through Him who gives me strength.**"*

What does Matthew 6:25-34 mean to you?

_____
_____
_____

† ***Seeking God first positions you for the***

BEST things in life.

When I was in college, the "perfect man" asked me to marry him. He was charming, handsome and rich. He even taught Bible study at his church. He seemed to be everything a girl would want in a husband.

But **I said no because I didn't feel my God saying yes.** And I'm so glad! God brought the man of *His* choice into my life soon after that, and no earthly mansion the other man offered me could compare to the love and adventures we've experienced carrying the Good News together to the ends of the earth.

† ***Surrendering to God is to your advantage.***

If you are truly seeking God's will, you are not likely to miss it. How do I know that? Because Jeremiah 29:13 says, *"You will seek Me and find Me, when you search for Me with all your heart."* It's a promise you can count on!

But what if your heart confuses you and you want something so badly you think God wants it for you too? What if you make a colossal mistake you end up regretting for the rest of your life?

God is STILL in control. His purposes for you still stand: *to know Him and enjoy Him and bring Him glory.*

Nothing surprises God; not even the messes you make. He knows what you're going to do long before you do it. And He already has a plan to use everything for good if you want to follow Him. Romans 8:28.

God is bigger than your messes.

A nice car, a great career and a beautiful wife are all things that can "break down" at any moment. But loving God and following

Him will bring joy, peace and meaning to every trial as you draw all the closer to Christ and become more than a conqueror. Romans 8:37-39.

† *Look for what God has for you instead of what you think you want, and you will find HE is all you need.*

If Jesus is your First Love, then His desires are your desires, and any other blessings are like sauce on steak: They won't satisfy your hunger — only the "steak" can do that — but they make loving Him all the richer. Psalm 34:8.

No one gets everything he wants in this life, except the man whose desire is for God. Then God will most certainly satisfy him with Himself.

What do you want for your future?

_____
_____
_____
_____

Is there anything you need or want that you worry about not having? Good grades? The right wife? A good career? God's will and purpose for your life? Explain.

_____
_____
_____
_____

What does Jeremiah 29:11-13 say about God's plans for you?

_____

God already has a perfect plan for your life. The Sovereign One who created you, Who loves you with no boundaries, has already planned for you the BEST …
HIMSELF!

"Delight yourself also in the Lord, and He shall give you the desires of your heart." Psalm 37:4

Read back through the statements and scriptures in italics in this chapter and highlight or circle the ones that especially impacted you.

Now, write a prayer handing your desires and your future over to God.

_____
_____
_____
_____
_____
_____
_____
_____
_____
_____
_____
_____

"For me, to live is Christ…"
Philippians 1:21a

1

Get in the Habit

of seeking God first. Let Him be the One you want more than anything else, and He will bless you as He guides you into His perfect plans for your life. Then even when the hardships hit, you will come out more than a conqueror through His love. Romans 8:37-39.

2Chapter

DARE

to be content

Genies aside ...

Write about a time when you expected or hoped something would happen, but it didn't turn out the way you wanted. How did that feel?

_____

_____

_____

_____

What if you hope for a great job making lots of money, but ten years from now find yourself employed as a garbage collector?

A friend of mine who delivered pizzas for a living actually felt *called by God* to that job. Every day he shared Christ's love with home-alone children, families in turmoil, lonely people. Then at the end of the day he took leftover pizzas to the homeless.

Providing for his wife and four children on a poverty-level salary was difficult, but God gave them endless opportunities to share Christ's love with other needy people in their low-income neighborhood.

Read 1 Timothy 6:6-11. How can desire for money be dangerous?

_____

_____

What should you pursue instead?

_____

_____

This is not to say you shouldn't work hard and do well in life. God may call you to be a successful businessman and live in a mansion. All I'm saying is:

The job you have and how many things you have should not be the source of your joy.
Hebrews 13:5-6.

The only treasures that last are eternal ones—intimacy with Christ, faith, love, salvation, joy, peace, heaven....

*"Do not lay up for yourselves treasures on earth, where moth and rust destroy and where thieves break in and steal; but lay up for yourselves treasures in heaven, where neither moth nor rust destroys and where thieves do not break in and steal. For **where your treasure is, there your heart will be also.**"* Matthew 6:19-21

Grab hold of the freedom and joy of knowing that **the God who loves you is in control.**

He knows your past, He knows your future, and He knows what you're going through now.

He has a plan, *and it's a good one.* Romans 8:28. He loves you. And *that's a peaceful place to rest.*

† **With God, even the hard times can be filled with joy and fulfillment.**

In Hosea 2:14-23, God led the Israelites into a desert, a Valley of "Trouble" (Achor).

As He spoke tenderly through their hard times, that place of troubles became a door of _____. (v. 15) Their view of God transformed through those hard times. They stopped calling Him "Master" (Baal), and called Him _____. (v. 16)

What does that mean to you? Isaiah 54:5.

_____

_____

_____

_____

Life's deserts bubble with refreshing springs when we lean on the God we love.
Psalm 42, Song of Songs 8:5.

Read Deuteronomy 32:10-11. What else

does God do with us in the desert?

_____

_____

_____

_____

The Hebrew word for "shield" also means to "surround" and "change direction."

If you look to the Lord, the Almighty One who loves you and surrounds you like a shield in the hard times (rather than looking at how bad your circumstances are) *that "desert" place can become a life-changing experience.*

What are some things you want but don't have? Write a prayer handing those things over to God and asking Him what He wants. Listen for His voice in answer to your surrender. He may give you a verse, lift your burden or fill you with peace. Pray back to Him whatever you feel Him saying. Write that prayer here.

_____

_____

_____

_____

_____

_____

_____

_____

God speaks in many ways. (See Chapter 12.) As you're learning to tune in to His voice, the most important way to position yourself to hear Him is to *surrender*: **Give up your own ideas and desires, and ask Him for His.**

Don't worry if you feel you can't hear Him clearly just yet. He may want to take you through different situations and grow you into understanding His answers.

But if your heart is surrendered to God, you won't miss out on any of the amazing adventures He has planned for your life.

NOW, WHAT DO I DO? HE SAYS HE ALREADY HAS EVERYTHING HE WANTS!

2

Get in the Habit

of handing everything over to God and resting in His Sovereignty. Isaiah 30:15. Surrender to Him, knowing you can trust Him, even if the outcome isn't what you expected. Whatever God is doing, it is GOOD because He is good.

3 Chapter

DARE

~ to fix your eyes on Jesus

Run for your life!

Imagine you're running a race. You've trained for this. Your plan is to win. The prize is a million dollars.

The weather is perfect—a cloud cover, a slight breeze. The track is level. You're running at a good pace thinking, *"I can do this!"*

But then the sun breaks through the clouds and something sparkles on the track. It looks like ... Yes, it must be. A *penny!* You stop, bend down, and pick it up.

You would never do that, would you? But unfortunately, many runners in this "race" of life (1 Corinthians 9:24, Acts 20:24, 2 Timothy 4:7) have missed out on the Grand Prize because something less worthy distracted them.

A good runner must fix his eyes on what he's running for and run undistracted.

A "penny" in this case could be **something you want that blocks you from taking hold of the better** (like riches, fame, pornography, sex, video games, movies or anything else that fills your mind and time).

Is anything you're reaching for taking you off-track? Stop a minute to ask the Lord and write what comes to mind.

_____

_____

_____

Busyness that keeps you from the Word and from your quiet times with God can also sidetrack you—like a runner more concerned with what's going on in the sidelines than with winning.

Has anything kept you so busy you haven't done the things that really matter? Ask God and write what comes to mind.

_____

_____

_____

Another way to slow your pace is to look at other runners and **compare** or **judge**.

But running well is something athletes *grow* into. They develop spiritual "muscles" through daily "exercise" (spending time with the Lord and following His lead through difficult situations). So don't worry if you think you don't run as well as someone else. And don't look down on others you think aren't running fast enough. Just trust in God's personalized training program to grow you and take you where you need to be at just the pace He has for you.

This journey is your own and the race is to draw closer to Jesus, not to look up or down at others. So don't let **pride** slow you down if you're doing well or **jealousy**, **discouragement** or **low self-esteem** if you're not. If you're busy focusing on yourself or others' issues, you'll miss what you're running for.

The only way to get the Prize is to *fix your eyes on Jesus.*

*"Let us **throw off everything that hinders ...** and **run with perseverance** the race marked out for us, **fixing our eyes on Jesus**."*
Hebrews 12:1b-2a (NIV)

Have you ever seen a runner in the Olympics carry an anvil? Of course not. But **wrong thought processes** weigh us down. 2 Corinthians 10:3-5, John 8:42-47.

What if you're not so sure God is good? Or that He hears your prayers? How might **doubt** affect how fast you run toward Him?

_____

_____

Have you ever wanted to tell someone about Jesus, but you were **afraid** to? Why?

_____

_____

_____

What if you feel God leading you to take a leadership position, but others criticize you and your friend gets angry because you don't hang out with him anymore. At last, too **discouraged** to go on, you quit.

Wrong thought processes slow you down when you're **looking at how incapable you are instead of how powerful your God is.** Philippians 4:13.

Pause a moment and think about that. Is there any situation in which you're relying on your own ability and coming up short? Hand that over to God now.

_____

_____

_____

Worry is another thought-line that depletes our energy. What does 1 Peter 5:7 say you should do with your burdens?

_____

_____

Is there anything you've been worried about? Ask God and write what comes to mind, handing it to Him.

_____

_____

_____

The past can load you down with extra "baggage" too.

If you often react out of self-defense, impatience, fear, anger, self-protection, self-pity or some other negative attitude outside the fruit of the Spirit (Galatians 5:1, 22-25), then you'll need the Lord's help to take that baggage from you. (See Chapter 22.)

You might think you've locked your emotions up tightly, but after you hit a few bumps and that lid pops off, you just might find your junk spilling out for all to see.

Are you carrying around something from the past you wish never happened? Are there ways in which you're still trying to cover it up or protect yourself? Explain.

_____

_____

_____

Do you struggle with **depression**, **anxiety**, **fear** or **panic attacks**? What thoughts lead you down that detour?

_____

_____

_____

Don't just let your mind wander anywhere it wants to go. Recognize the thought processes that slow you down and block your view of Jesus. 2 Corinthians 10:3-5.

Just because you believe something doesn't mean it's true. Only what God says is true. John 8:42-47.

Surrender all your opinions, ideas, viewpoints, hopes, dreams, fears and worries over to Jesus. Ask Him what He has to say about every thought you think. Realign your thoughts with God's Word (See Chapter 22), thank Him for every blessing He's given you, and get back on track.

Let God's truth become yours.

3

Get in the Habit

of fixing your eyes on Jesus and throwing off everything that weighs you down. Notice what distracts you, hand those thoughts to Jesus, ask Him for His, and get back on track.

Chapter 4

DARE

~ to run unhindered

Want to run faster?

*"Let us lay aside every weight, and the **sin which so easily ensnares us**, and let us run with endurance the race that is set before us, **looking unto Jesus**, the Author and Finisher of our faith."* Hebrews 12:1b-2a

One day, I saw a youth running from the police. His baggy pants hung so low (to show his underwear in the current style of that day) that they kept slipping down to his knees and tripping him up. Finally, he landed on his face!

Any runner would be a fool to wear pants like that. And yet, sometimes our **sin** and **wrong choices** entangle us just like that youth.

Have you ever felt ensnared by sin? How did it affect your peace? Your joy? Your relationship with God and others?

_____

_____

_____

Everyone makes mistakes.

But *the one who fixes his eyes on Jesus grows through his mistakes* and RUNS FASTER.

1 John 1:9 says, *"If we confess our sins, He is faithful and just to forgive us our sins and to cleanse us from all unrighteousness."*

Line your race track with that truth, and if ever you do trip and fall, you won't have to worry about the ground opening up to swallow you in a muddy pit of **guilt** and **condemnation**. Romans 8:1.

The key to running unhindered is to fix your eyes on Jesus.

If He is your first love, your one passion, then temptation will lose its appeal next to the joy of running toward Him.

This whole race is about relationship, after all, not works. So, don't just try to *will* yourself to do the right thing, although your will to follow Christ is most certainly crucial. It's just not *enough*. You need Someone stronger.

Seek to fall deeper in love with Jesus. Then His love in you and your passion for Him will fuel your will to come in line with His. Romans 8:35-39.

Colossians 3:8 tells us to "take off" **anger**. What are ways anger leads us to more sin?

_____

_____

Most anger comes from pride and **unforgiveness**. What does Matthew 6:15 say?

_____

_____

Unforgiveness can cost us the race.

What is the time frame Ephesians 4:26-27 gives us to forgive and be done with anger before the enemy gets a "foothold" on us?

_____

_____

If you go to sleep on your anger, the next morning you might think you're over it, but that's just because it's not at the surface anymore. Buried anger ferments into **bitterness**. Ephesians 4:31. And bitterness into **depression** and thoughts of suicide; and that's just one example of how sin will be the death of you. James 1:14-15.

Which character in the cartoon do you feel most like? Why? _____

_____

Look through the sins and wrong thought

processes bolded and underlined in these last two chapters. Is there anything weighing you down? Explain.

_____

_____

_____

Ask the Lord which items the second cartoon character is struggling with most resemble your issues and why. Write what comes to mind. _____

_____

_____

_____

Still in prayer, letting your love for God and His love for you lead your thoughts, picture yourself handing to Jesus the things that hinder you one by one. Write your prayer here.

_____

_____

_____

_____

What is He giving you in return? Ask Him. Write what you feel Him showing you.

_____

_____

_____

_____

"Everyone who competes for the prize (does) it to obtain a perishable crown, but we for an imperishable crown." 1 Corinthians 9:25

⤞ 4 ⤝

Get in the habit

of asking God what sin and wrong thought processes hinder you from running after Him. Hand those to Him, asking for forgiveness. Picture Him taking each one from you and handing you something beautiful and eternal in return. Grab that and run with it!

Chapter 5

DARE

to know who you are in Christ

Wear the right hat!

Did you know that when you chose to follow Christ, your identity changed? *"You are no longer a slave but a son, and if a son, then an heir of God through Christ."* Galatians 4:7.

From slave to prince and heir to a kingdom! That just doesn't happen on this earth. But God's kingdom operates by different standards. 1 Corinthians 1:26-31.

*Most people receive their identity through what they do, but **your identity is found in what Christ has done for you.***

Belonging to the Kingdom of God means a *change in your loyalties.* 2 Corinthians 5:17.

In other words, you no longer do things like those you hang out with do. Nor do you do things according to the culture you grew up in or live in. *You are an "alien" now.*

Not the kind with spindly arms and green skin. That's just in the movies. But you *are* extra-terrestrial in a sense. *Heaven is your home now.* 1 Peter 1:17; 2:11-12.

That means **you do things the way *Jesus* does, not the way others think you should.**

For example, say you're heading up a team to organize a youth event and one of the guys helping you isn't keeping his commitments.

Do you…

1. Talk about the problem, but not to him?
2. Compare him to someone else to shame him into doing the right thing?
3. Talk around the subject, hoping he guesses your meaning?
4. Get someone else to talk to him about it?
5. Speak harshly and threaten him?
6. Confront him in front of others?

Each of these reactions is actually protocol in certain cultures. Even in the same country, cultures vary from north to south, east to west or family to family. *A guy could wear himself out dancing to so many tunes!*

But what does Galatians 1:10 say?

_____

_____

Only God's opinion matters. And *you please Him already just because you're His.*

So, **take every piece of advice to Him, and** *measure it with His Word and His heart of love* (Matthew 22:37-40) **before you receive it.**

THANKS, BUT THIS IS THE HAT I'M WEARING!

You are who GOD says you are, not what others say or think about you.

Let's look back at that situation with the slacker. What would you do as the leader?

_____

_____

What would Jesus do? See Matthew 18:15, Ephesians 4:15, and Mark 10:35-45.

_____

_____

The world makes decisions based on what others expect of them, what seems best, personal gain, fear, low self-esteem, or any number of other thoughts, urges, or emotions.

But *you are a prince, heir to the Kingdom.*

You make decisions based on your King's lordship over your life.

A boss or friend may urge you to do what's acceptable by the world's standards. But if it goes against your King's commands, graciously decline. Whatever you "lose" on earth is worth it for the eternal rewards. 2 Corinthians 4:17-18, Philippians 3:7-8.

What are some other things in the culture you live in that clash with Kingdom Culture?

_____

_____

_____

_____

In addition to the stress to conform, Satan loves to use life experiences to convince you to agree with his lies. *Stand on the truth.*

Throw Romans 8:37 in his face next time you feel like a failure. Stick him with 1 Corinthians 1:26-30 whenever he tells you you're nothing or you're stupid. Stand on Hebrews 10:14 and Romans 8:1 whenever you feel you don't measure up. Declare Philippians 4:13 next time you feel you can't do anything right.

Take a moment to write two columns in your journal. At the top of the left column, write "Lies," and at the top of the right, write "Truth." Walk through the above paragraph and write the lies on the left and the truth on the right.

Have you ever struggled with any of those lies? What other lies do you struggle with? Write them in the left column, and ask Jesus for the truth. Write any verses or anything else He shows you in the right column.

What do the following verses say about who you are in Christ?

John 15:15: *I am <u>Jesus' friend</u>* _____

1 Corinthians 6:19: *I am* _____

1 Corinthians 12:27: *I am* _____

Hebrews 10:14: *I am* _____

Galatians 5:13: *I am* _____

Psalm 103:12: *I am* _____

Ephesians 2:10: *I am* _____

1 Corinthians 3:9: *I am* _____

Acts 1:8: *I am* _____

Matthew 5:14: *I am* _____

2 Corinthians 5:20: *I am* _____

Ephesians 2:19: *I am* _____

Prayerfully read those over again and mark the ones you feel God especially speaking to your heart. Write them in your journal.

Get in the habit

of walking out in the truth of who you are in Christ. If you're Jesus' friend, then talk with Him, hang out with Him, know He's with you everywhere you go and that He's FOR you. If you're His Son, then take on His character in the way you speak and act.

to know Who your Father is

The perfect Dad

What kind of father would you like to be?

_____

_____

_____

I was blessed to grow up with a father who loved me lavishly. No matter what happened, I could crawl up into his lap and feel safe.

Keeping up with my energetic older brother meant a lot of hard knocks, but my father picked me up when I fell, wiped my tears and bandaged my wounds.

My doctor dad gave generously to missions and took care of inner city poor people where we lived in the United States.

Then one day his friend challenged him, "If we who care don't go, who will?" And that was that. God called him to a Third World country to provide medical care for those who had none, and I grew up helping him on mobile clinic trips into the jungle.

Just like any family, we had our many problems. But my father often asked forgiveness for the things he did wrong and always pointed back to God as the Perfect One.

Why am I sharing this with you? Because not only is it helpful to know what a man of God looks like as you're seeking to become one yourself, but **the way we see our earthly fathers greatly influences the way we see God.**

Look at my story again and underline key themes that might have helped shape that little girl's view of her Heavenly Father.

Even as God used my earthly father to show me His love, the enemy often uses negative experiences to build arguments against God's character. 2 Corinthians 10:3-5.

For example,

⊙ A physically or emotionally abused child might see God as an imposing judge ready to punish the slightest mistake.

⊙ A son whose father was absent or too busy to spend time with him might think God is disinterested or not there for him.

⊙ The child of a critical father might struggle with the need to earn God's favor.

⊙ And a son whose father broke promises might not trust God.

Of course, it doesn't always turn out that way. Some children pull through traumatic childhoods leaning on God all the more.

But what was your childhood like? How has your father influenced the way you see God? Ask the Lord and write what comes to mind.

_____

_____

_____

_____

Everything we believe and think must agree with what God says or we could be listening to a different father—the father of _____. John 8:42-47.

So, it's important to know what God your Father is truly like. Pray through each scripture below and describe Him. Pause whenever you feel Him touching your heart and meditate on that God-quality, writing notes in the margin if you like.

† Mark 10:13-16 _____

_____

† Isaiah 40:11 _____

_____

† 1 John 4:16 _____

_____

† 1 John 1:9 _____

† Deuteronomy 31:8 ______

† Deuteronomy 33:27 ______

† Psalm 86:15 ______

† Psalm 27:10 ______

† Psalm 68:5 ______

† 1 Peter 5:7 ______

† John 14:23 ______

Look back now at the bulleted childhoods on the facing page and also your own. Which truths about God knock down those lies? Draw arrows from truth to lie, scribbling out the lie as truth conquers it. Here's some added ammunition:

- † ***Your Father loves you.*** 1 John 3:1a.
- † ***He is good.*** Psalm 142:7, Psalm 103.
- † ***He cares for you.*** Matthew 7:7-11, Jeremiah 29:11.
- † ***He is for you.*** Psalm 25, 139:7-10.
- † ***He fights for you.*** Isaiah 42:10-17.
- † ***He knows His plans for you, and they are good.*** Jeremiah 29:11.
- † ***He holds you up so you don't fall.*** Psalm 37:23-24.

Is there anything you need to forgive your earthly father for? Will you do that now? (See Chapter 37.)

"I forgive my dad for ______

______."

Spend some time in prayer for your father, your family and yourself. Ask God to build in you now the qualities He wants you to have as a father. Use Ephesians 3:16-21 as your guide, if you like, and write your prayer here:

______

That hole in your heart that longs for the perfect father is God-sized.

Release your father to not be God and ***God to be your Father.***

6

Get in the Habit

of tearing down every argument that sets itself up against the knowledge of God.
2 Corinthians 10:3-5.

Make sure you see God as He truly is, not as the enemy would like you to see Him. Trust God. He loves you and is for you. He will never leave you or forsake you. He is the perfect father you long for. Your earthly father will never be able to fill that hole in your heart. So forgive him and release him from your expectations. Then expect God to fill that void with perfect love like only the perfect Father can give.

7hapter

DARE

to walk in intimacy with Christ

Higher up and deeper in

Life can be a bit of a bungee jump sometimes, don't you think? Have you ever felt like you were plummeting off a cliff head first into some terrible situation?

There is a way to bounce back without dashing on the rocks.

By placing your faith in the "cords" of God's love (Hosea 11:3-4), difficult situations transform into thrilling ones and your relationship with Christ tightens.

With God, a problem is not a problem. It is an *opportunity*.

I've been through some tough things in life, but I wouldn't trade them for anything! I've come to find *the more difficult the trial, the more spectacular Jesus is*, and the more I fall in love with Him.

In fact, those hard times have been the very things He has used to set me free from whatever heart issues made my problems so problematic in the first place.

But to go through battles in life as "more than a conqueror," you need to tighten that cord around you—*your relationship with Christ*. Romans 8:37-39.

If you don't, you'll end up like so many Christians who dash upon the same rocks over and over because they didn't hang onto God the first time. They waste every thrilling opportunity for higher heights and deeper depths with Him by getting angry at Him, avoiding Him or blaming Him and others for their sin and wrong choices.

Have you ever done that before? Explain.

_____

_____

So, how do you tighten that cord?

"Draw near to God, and He will draw near to you." James 4:8.

It's as simple as that. John 15:1-17 talks about being God's friend. That means sharing the secrets of your heart with Him, even as He shares His with you. 1 Corinthians 4:1.

You see, you were made for relationship with the God who loves you and formed you for Himself. He created you to enjoy His love and love Him back.

"I am in My Father, and you in Me, and I in you. He who has My commandments and keeps them, it is he who loves Me. And he who loves Me will be loved by My Father, and I will love him and manifest Myself to him."
John 14:20-21

The secret to intimacy is a passionate love for God.

When you fall in love, you can't stop thinking about that girl you've fallen for. You long to be near her and hear her voice. You love the things she loves. You even take on opinions and ideas she feels passionately about…

In a way, that's what it's like to have a passion for God. **You want to be one with Him** (John 15-17), to know Him so deeply and so well that you take on His viewpoints, His interests, His heart, His character. He's with you all the time, so your conversations never end.

Nothing else matters in life but Christ.

Let Jesus be your first thought when you wake: *"Lord, what do You want to do today?"*… your last thought as you sleep: *"Lord, talk to me in my dreams"*… and all your thoughts in between: *"Lord, this is hard. Help me. … Give me the words to speak to this person. … What a beautiful sunset You just made. …"*

A tree with a taproot of passion for God will dig down deep to draw life from the rivers of His love and produce spiritual fruit aplenty.

Check out the basketful in Galatians 5:22-25. **The closer you walk with Christ, the more abundant and meaningful your life will be.** John 10:10b.

When our children were babies, I lived in continual exhaustion. In fact, nearly every day when I put them down for a nap, I fell asleep. I didn't mean to, because I was hungry for God and it was my only time to be alone with Him, but I just couldn't help it.

That longing in my heart to be with the Lord drew God close, even as I slept. He often awakened me with dreams of how much He loves me. But one time, I actually heard His voice *audibly.* He said, *"Come!"*

I awoke with a start. Twice more He called out to me, *"Come. Come!"*

I don't know about you, but I think I probably imagined that if God were to speak to me audibly, He would boom in some deep voice something like, "I'm calling you to the so-and-so people of such-and-such dark place to preach My Good News..."

But no. **He called me into His presence. He called me to Himself.**

So how important is intimacy with Christ? *It is what you were created for!*

But what if you don't feel passion for God?

Do you want to? Because that's a great place to start! Tell Him you *hunger to hunger* for more of Him, and then take steps to draw near, like the bulleted ones below. James 4:8. It's not as if He's going anywhere. He's been here all along, just waiting for you to notice.

Some **ways to draw near to God:**

† Daily quiet times alone with Him
† Private and corporate worship
† Prayer
† Listening to God
† Obedience
† Repentance
† Forgiving others
† Loving others
† Surrender
† Humility
† A thankful heart
† Knowing His Word
† Walking in Truth
† Spending time with those close to God
† Teaching others about God

Today, talk with God through each situation you face. Ask Him what He's doing so you can walk "in step" with Him. Proverbs 3:5-7, Galatians 5:25.

Then, at the end of the day, see how this day felt different from yesterday. Did He show you something you might not have noticed if you hadn't been talking with Him?

_____
_____
_____

Tomorrow when you wake, make Jesus your first thought again. Hand Him your day, and ask Him what He wants to do with it.

7

Get in the Habit ...

... of handing Jesus every day before it even starts and looking for Him all throughout the day. Share with Him your thoughts and listen for His answers. If you walk in the intimacy with Christ you were created for, every moment will pulsate with purpose, meaning and JOY.

Part 2

"For this reason I bow my knees to the Father ... that He would grant you, according to the riches of His glory, to be strengthened with might through His Spirit in the inner man, that Christ may dwell in your hearts through faith; that you, being rooted and grounded in love, may be able to comprehend with all the saints what is the width and length and depth and height—to know the love of Christ which passes knowledge; that you may be filled with all the fullness of God."

Ephesians 3:16-19

Deeper In

Chapter 8

DARE

to enter the Secret Place

Where eagles fly

If you could be a superhero, which special powers would you want and why?

_____

_____

Deep within most of us is a longing to be more than just the average guy. We want to make a difference, to be a hero, to defy evil, win the fight, save the world.... Or *maybe we just want to fly*.

Why? Because y*ou really were created for powerful things.* You're not just some slightly dorky Clark Kent who can't seem to speak up for himself or get the girl. *You really are an alien. Heaven is your home, and within you is the power to overcome the evil one who is out to destroy this world.* Luke 10:19, John 16:33, 1 John 4:4, 5:4-5.

But if you're distracted by your earthly identity and problems, you'll forget who you really are and what you're here for. You'll strive in your own strength and wear yourself out. You might even fight the wrong enemy and miss what the war was all about!

In order to be and do all the mighty things your Father wants to empower you for, you need to go to that "Secret Citadel" where He's waiting to meet with you. He even gave you a map to get there:

> *"But you, when you pray, go into your room, and when you have shut your door, **pray to your Father who is in the Secret Place**."*
> Matthew 6:6

The Secret Place is where you rest from the battle. Where you commune with your Heavenly Father. Where He teaches you and trains you to get ready for the difficulties that lie ahead. Where He empowers you to conquer the enemy. Where He tells you how to "get the girl" (that amazing woman of God He has prepared for you, see Chapter 39). *And it's also where you learn to fly.*

> *"As an eagle stirs up its nest, hovers over its young, spreading out its wings, taking them up, carrying them on its wings, so the Lord alone led him."* Deuteronomy 32:11-12

In the Secret Place, our Father lifts us up on His wings to see His Eagle-eye viewpoint of our problems so we can *soar over them.* Isaiah 40:31. In Exodus 19:4, what is our destination?

_____.

Are you feeling superhero-ish yet? Because we're not finished yet. What can this Power within you do? Luke 1:37, Philippians 4:13.

_____

What does that include? John 14:12-14.

_____

_____

Do you believe that? Why or why not?

_____

_____

When we walk as one with Christ in the power of His Spirit, the sky is the limit. The lost can be saved, the blind see, the lame walk, the dead rise again, *the world change ....*

But **the greatest miracle of all will be what He does in your own heart.**

Resting in the Secret Place, we can listen to our Father, take on His viewpoints, and be transformed and *empowered by His Spirit.*

Jesus is our Model. How did He get alone with His Father? John 5:19-20, Luke 5:16.

_____

Like your King, you also have a "Fortress of Solitude" where you can go to be renewed and empowered to face your archenemy and win. **Skip that time with your Father, and you won't soar over problems;** *you'll crash and burn.* Matthew 7:24-27.

If you're still not quite sure **how to have powerful quiet times**, try following Jesus' sample prayer in Matthew 6:9-15:

† Worship God. (v 9)

† Surrender to His will and His Kingdom purposes in your heart and life. Ask Him to bring about the things of heaven here on this earth, *even through you.* (v 10)

† Trust Him to supply all your needs. (v 11)

† Admit your sin and ask forgiveness. (v 12)

† Forgive others. (v 12, 14-15)

† Look for God's paths through every trial, so you don't end up on enemy detours, falling to sin or fighting against your brothers instead of standing together with them against the real enemy. (v 13a)

† Bare your heart before God, so He can set you free from whatever snares the enemy sets for you (like anger, selfishness, depression, judgment, fear, loneliness, lust, etc.). Use the Galatians 5:22-23 Gauge in Chapter 22. (v 13b)

And don't forget to spend time in the Word, so your King can instruct you in living out what it says. Why is that important? John 8:31-32, Matthew 7:24-27.

_____

_____

Your time on earth is short and you have a purpose here. You can't afford to be distracted by the mundane, or your enemy will ensnare you with kryptonite lies and you may never see him coming. *You must know the Truth so the Truth will set you free.* John 8:32.

Has a busy schedule kept you from meeting with your Father in the Secret Place? What will you do to change that? Ask God and write what comes to mind.

_____

_____

*"Now to Him Who is able to do immeasurably more than all we ask or imagine, **according to His power that is at work within us**..."*
Ephesians 3:20.

Are you stressed out doing things in your own strength? Have earthly problems distracted you? Are you fitting into others' plans for you or God's? What needs to change for you to be empowered by His Spirit? Ephesians 3:20. Ask God and write what He shows you.

_____

_____

_____

_____

You don't have to fall when you can fly.

*"But those who (trust in) the Lord shall renew their strength; **they shall mount up with wings like eagles**, they shall run and not be weary, they shall walk and not faint."* Isaiah 40:31

Does that describe you? Or are you feeling worn out? Do you feel like the enemy is defeating you and those you love? *Get into the Secret Place and seek the One Whose power triumphs over all!* Psalm 91:1.

 8

Get in the habit

of a daily quiet time with God. In fact, plan a time once a week or once a month to spend half a day or a whole day alone with Him. You were made for more than the mundane. You were made to be a conduit for His power. Let Him use you to make a difference in this world.

Chapter 9

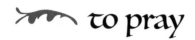

DARE to pray

A friend in high places

Imagine you're stalked by a dangerous thief whose intent is to destroy you.

Hope isn't lost, though, because you're well connected. With just one punch of a call button, *a whole army will fight for you!*

"That's nice," you say, as you put that call button on a shelf in the closet.

The thief blasts into your house in a surprise attack. You head for the closet, but he grabs you by the heels and drags you down, beating you to a pulp. You try to defend yourself, but you're too weak. In the end he carries away all the things you love most, leaving you in a defeated heap on the floor.

Don't you wish you'd hit that button?

You really do have a thief bent on destroying you, but your connection with the King of Kings makes you more than a conqueror. John 10:10, Romans 8:31-39. **Prayer is your call button.** So, as you can imagine…

The enemy's main aim is to stop you from praying.

He may club you with busyness, slice you with ridicule, slam you with anger at God, strangle you with self-pity or dry quiet times.

But whatever his methods,

Prayerlessness will destroy your intimacy with Christ and make you powerless to walk in the "better" things.

Prayer tunes us in to God's viewpoint so we can see what He's doing and join Him there.

When we pray, we position ourselves to submit to God's ways and defeat the enemy's plans. In fact, **whenever we pray God's will Satan loses ground.**

So how do you know what God's will is? *Through His Word.* **Anything God does or asks you to do will always agree with His Word,** not just a tiny portion of it, but *all of it.* (See the Three-Fold Sieve for knowing God's voice in Chapter 13.)

One powerful way, then, to partner with God in agreeing with His purposes and calling them forth into the world around you is to *pray Scripture.*

For example, if you want to pray for protection over you and others, Psalm 91 is a great start. What does verse 1 say about the Secret Place we talked about last chapter? What are some ways He keeps us safe? (v. 2-16) How might you write that psalm into a prayer?

_____

_____

_____

_____

Living in a spiritually dark country, our family prayed a version of that passage every night, asking God to fill our home with His presence and surround us with His angels, guarding us and our things from any harm.

When a business moved in next door, they parked their vehicles in our carport instead of theirs. When we asked them why, they said, "Because when we park them in ours they get stolen, but when we park them in yours they don't." Why do you think that is?

_____

_____

What situation do you know of needs prayer? Ask God for His heart on the matter. If a passage doesn't come to mind, try doing a Word Search (Chapter 22), looking up key words in a concordance, letting God point you to the verses that apply, and writing them into a prayer here. _____

_____

_____

_____

_____

In Ephesians 6:18, prayer is not just for the Secret Place; it's for *every moment:*

*"**Pray in the Spirit on all occasions** with all kinds of prayers and requests. With this in mind, be alert, and **always keep on praying**."*

I like to start my mornings with prayer even before I get out of bed, handing my day over to God and asking Him what He wants to do with it. Throughout the day, I **pray and listen for His leading before making decisions.** If I don't, *I'll miss the miracles!*

God is always doing something amazing. *Prayer gives me a front-row seat and positions me to be used by Him.*

God is God, and He can do anything He wants any time. But **He most often waits for us to pray before He acts.** *He doesn't just want to get something done; He wants to do something **with us and in us.***

Prayer releases the power of God upon the earth. Revelation 5:8; 8:3-5.

Imagine you're a soldier in an army and enemy archers are raising their bows to shoot.

Do you scatter, leaving each man to fend for himself? You could. Maybe your shield would keep you safe for a while.

But what if your army bands together with the front row kneeling, shields before them, and the back row holding shields above? Bonded together in prayers of faith, your army becomes a united front the enemy can't penetrate. Ephesians 6:10-18, Philippians 1:27-28.

Prayer unites us with God and with others.

In your journal today, make two columns, the left with prayer requests, and the right blank for now. As God answers your prayers, write what He did in the right column and date each answer.

"Whatever things you ask in prayer, believing, you will receive."
Matthew 21:22

 9

Get in the Habit

of praying all throughout the day. Ask God what He's doing so you can join Him there. In fact, make your whole life a prayer to Him.

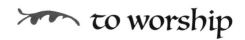 to worship

Because He is worthy

Within you is a God-sized hole that can only be filled with knowing God personally, feeling His great love for you, loving Him back, bringing Him glory as you love others through His love, and *worshipping* Him.

Worship is what you were created for.

What are some of God's many names in the Word that show His greatness and love?

1 Peter 4:19 _____

Deuteronomy 33:27 _____

Jeremiah 16:19 _____

Isaiah 54:5 _____

Genesis 16:13 _____

Exodus 15:26b _____

Other _____

Other _____

How has God personally demonstrated some of those aspects of His character to you?

_____
_____
_____
_____
_____

Sometimes we can get so preoccupied with how big our problems are we forget **how big our God is.** But when we *fix our eyes on Him,* our worries shrink in the light of His power and glory.

Worshipping God transforms both you and what you're going through.

Write about a time when you worshipped and felt God's presence near. How did that experience affect you?

_____

_____
_____
_____

Humbly recognizing God as Sovereign and bowing before Him in worship places you in the flow of His leading. Not only will peace fill your heart and serving Him become more important to you than the outcome of your trial, but He may even give you just the instructions you need to overcome. Or change the situation altogether. He is Almighty, after all.

Worship is powerful.

What do these verses tell you about the power of worship?

Isaiah 30:32: _____

_____

2 Chronicles 20:21-22: _____

_____

Exodus 23:25-27: _____

_____

1 Samuel 16:23: _____

_____

When we worship God, **Satan's plans are defeated.** He is no match for the Almighty! Not by a long shot. In fact, **Satan himself must bow to the King of Kings.** Philippians 2:10.

Worship is a winning strategy against the enemy.

Have you ever had a nightmare or woken up in a panic? **Worship invites God near and makes the enemy flee.**

David knew the power of praise as warfare. Psalm 18. In fact, nearly every one of his psalms that begins with how terrible his enemy is ends with how great his God is.

But David loved the Lord too much to just worship whenever he was afraid; *he wor-*

shipped Him with his life. Acts 13:22.

➤➤ ***Worship isn't just something we do on Sunday mornings. It is a lifestyle.***

Picture worship in the shape of a cross, like the illustration below. The vertical beam is you bringing God glory through praising Him in your quiet times or with others. The horizontal beam is you bringing God glory as you walk out your faith into daily life, living each moment for Him.

"Oh come, let us **sing** to the Lord! Let us **shout joyfully** to the Rock of our salvation. Let us come before His presence with **thanksgiving**; let us shout joyfully to Him with **psalms**. For *the LORD is the great God, and the great King above all gods. In His hand are the deep places of the earth; the heights of the*

hills are His also. The sea is His, for He made it; and His hands formed the dry land. Oh come, let us worship and **bow down**; Let us **kneel** before the Lord our Maker. For *He is our God, and we are the people of His pasture, and the sheep of His hand."* Psalm 95:1-7

What are some ways to worship God? See the **bolded** words in the passage above, and add others that come to mind. How do you like to worship God?

_____
_____
_____
_____

Why do we worship God? See the *italics* in the verses above, and add your own reasons.

_____
_____
_____
_____

What are some ways you can worship God through how you live your life?

_____
_____
_____
_____

Spend time in worship today. Listen to your favorite praise music, play an instrument, tell God how wonderful He is, write Him a poem or letter, paint Him a picture, lie prostrate before Him, raise your hands, dance — whatever you want to do to worship One so worthy.

Write your experience with Him in your journal. Then walk out of the Secret Place purposing to live each moment as if bowed at His feet.

➤➤ 10 ➤➤

Get in the Habit
of worshipping God in your daily quiet times and in your mind and heart all the time. Live every moment as if bowed at Christ's feet.

Chapter 11

DARE

~ to experience God

Inviting God near

Worship ushers in God's felt presence. It invites Him near and opens our hearts to experience Him in deep ways. 2 Chronicles 6-7.

As my friend and I prayed together in a dingy hotel room in the dark country where we live, we burst into spontaneous praise. Nothing fancy. No piano, no guitar, no hymnal. We didn't even sing. With grateful hearts, *we simply told the Lord how wonderful He is.*

The room filled with an awesome presence and I landed on my face on the grimy carpet. I could hear angel wings whirring above me and shout-songs of "Holy! Holy! Holy!"

When finally I dared to rise, I found my friend still sitting on her bed trembling, her eyes glazed over in wonder. "It was like huge hummingbird wings in my face," she said.

Is that experience hard to believe? Why?

_____

_____

There are actually editions of this book without that story because Christian leaders forbid me to tell it or to say the word "tremble" as a response to God's presence. Why do you think the enemy would want to cover up God's greatness and discourage fear of the Lord? James 2:19.

_____

_____

God doesn't fit in the boxes of human reasoning. His glory doesn't go away just because we weren't looking when He manifested it. He is GOD. All-Powerful. Almighty. And *worthy of our worship.*

Everything we believe about God must agree with His Word for it to be true.

So, let's look at what the Bible says about God's majesty and man's response. What did Isaiah experience in God's presence? How did he react? Isaiah 6.

_____

_____

_____

Can you think of other times in the Word when God revealed Himself in mighty ways to His people? How did He then empower them to do amazing things for His glory afterward?

_____

_____

_____

A worshipful life is a powerful life. And *that* is what the enemy is afraid of!

When we worship God and walk out of our quiet times empowered by His Spirit, we are more than conquerors through His love; *more powerful even than Satan.* Romans 8:37-39.

Worshipping God draws us near to Him. And fear of the Lord is a safe place. Psalm 2:11, Proverbs 29:25. But ***not bowing to God's majesty is dangerous.***

If you buy into Satan's arguments against knowing God, he just might use you to fight opposite God's truth and purposes, persecuting those who fear the Lord, love and obey Him, rather than joining together with them to oppose the real enemy. John 8:42-47, 2 Corinthians 10:3-5.

Remember, *just because you believe something doesn't make it true.* **Only what God says is true. *So know Who God is and believe Him only.***

When we worship God, we honor Him for

Who He is, and He delights in our praises.

God is intimate and personal, and every worship experience is unique and different. Occasionally, He meets us in obvious ways like He did in that hotel room. But more often,

His touch is so soft we must draw near Him to feel it. James 4:8a.

God wants followers who love Him — who long so desperately for Him *they seek Him with all their hearts.* Those are the ones who find Him. Jeremiah 29:11-14.

God loves to show His glory to those who long for Him. Exodus 33:17-23.

One day, as I read about how God showed up in miraculous ways at a church service somewhere in the United States, I had to put the book down. I didn't want to just read someone else's experiences; *I wanted my own.* So I headed out alone on a hike in the snowy wilderness asking God to show me His glory.

About a mile out, I was praying and enjoying God's creation when a pack of wolves stepped out of the forest and surrounded me.

I froze. "I wanted to *see* Your glory; not die and *go* to glory!" my mind screamed, as I begged God to spare my life.

Eventually, the wolves lost interest and disappeared back into the trees. I hurried up a rise toward safety, and as I reached the top of a ridge, the Lord's still small voice in my mind whispered, "Do you want to see My glory? Turn around."

I turned just in time to see the sunset light up the top of a mountain as if on fire.

Miraculous displays of God's glory are all around us all the time if we would but look for Him. Matthew 16:1-4.

But sometimes I get so caught up in how I want God to answer that I miss how He answered. I'd seen many sunsets more spectacular than that one. But what other unexpected way did God show me His glory in that snowy wilderness? _____
_____
_____

Have you ever expected God to do something in a certain way and He didn't? How did that make you feel? What did He do instead? If you're not sure, ask Him.

_____
_____
_____

Whether you feel God's touch when you worship or not, whether He answers your prayers the way you want Him to or not, *God is still worthy of worship.* Job 1:13-21; 13:15; Habakkuk 3:17-18. So *worship Him.*

Meditate on Psalm 135, and spend time in worship. Think about God's greatness. If He shows you a sin, repent. But also, just enjoy Him. Because worshipping God is what you were created for. Write your experience here.

_____
_____
_____
_____
_____
_____

"When He came near ... the whole crowd of disciples began joyfully to praise God in loud voices for all the miracles they had seen.... Some of the Pharisees in the crowd said to Jesus, 'Teacher, rebuke your disciples!'

"'I tell you,' He replied, 'if they keep quiet, the stones will cry out.'" Luke 19:37-40 (NIV)

 11

Get in the Habit
of drawing near to God so He will draw near to you. James 4:8. If you seek Him, He will make sure you find Him. Jeremiah 29:13.

12 Chapter

DARE

to listen to the Voice that counts

Tuning in to Truth

God is not a candy machine — put in just the right prayer and out pops the prize.

Prayer is a two-way conversation. It is a *relationship*. He wants to *talk with* you.

Do you believe that? Because so many Christians today don't. In fact, when I suggested to a group of missionaries that we pray first before making decisions or giving advice (Proverbs 3:5-7), they replied, "But if people listen to God they'll come up with all kinds of crazy things!" and "You just say that, Mikaela, because you believe God speaks."

If we listen to fear or doubt, we'll miss the Voice that counts. John 8:42-47.

"My sheep hear My voice, and I know them, and they follow Me." John 10:27

God's voice shakes things up.

What does Psalm 29 say to your heart?

_____

_____

_____

_____

When God speaks, He rocks my world! He doesn't just change me; *He changes my circumstances.*

One job God led me to placed me under three direct supervisors, as well as a higher boss who also liked to tell me what to do. Pleasing so many head-strong men at once wasn't easy, especially since obeying one often meant disobeying another; and because they didn't pray before making decisions, their commands often contradicted God's, as well.

I was faced with a dilemma. Obey God or obey man? And if I obey man, which one? Galatians 1:10, Hebrews 13:17.

I needed to listen to the Lord to know how to walk through the conflicting commands. Each time, God gave me specific instructions, and if I followed them exactly, He miraculously opened up loopholes I could slide through to obey both Him and my leaders. And I do mean *miraculously!*

I laughingly called Him "Lord of the Loopholes" during that time, and He called me His "undercover agent." Even though I had a job under earthly bosses, the One I truly worked for used me as His agent of love. Often His instructions included speaking truth and grace in the midst of lies and dissension.

Eventually He released me from that job, but what a ride we had together, and how His voice changed everything every time!

God's voice changes my perspective.

The Lord may not answer my prayers the way I want Him to, but *listening to Him changes how I feel* about my problem.

As I **lay all my opinions and ideas down at His feet**, He gives me His. And when I walk out in the fullness of what He's telling me to do, *He does amazing things*.

I love to **soak in His presence and in His Word, so His truth washes over me**, knocking down any lies I believe that make my situation worse and setting me free to see things His way and join Him in what He's doing.

I also **write what He's telling me in my journal or in the margins of my Bible**, so I can look back on His words and re-seal them in my heart.

God is speaking all the time.

The Bible tells us God speaks to us in many ways, including

† His Word (2 Timothy 3:16-17)
† Circumstances (2 Corinthians 12:7-10; Psalm 40:1-3)
† Others (1 Corinthians 2:4-13)
† His still small voice in our mind, heart (John 14:26, Psalm 42:8, Ezekial 18:1)
† Dreams and visions (Acts 2:17)
† Impressions or urgings (Acts 15:28)
† A sense of peace (Philippians 4:7)
† Signs and wonders (Acts 2:17-21)
† Nature (Psalm 125; 19:1-4)

Which of these are the most common ways God speaks to you? What other ways does God speak? Which ways would you like to experience more? Why?

_____

_____

_____

_____

Tell about a time you obeyed God. How did He speak to you? How did you know it was Him? What did He say? How did that affect your situation? How did He change you?

_____

_____

_____

_____

_____

When I was 13, I hungered for more of God. I had seen other Christians enjoying a joy like I'd never experienced, and I wanted what they had. So I stepped outside one night to be alone with the Lord. I pointed to a dim star and said, "Lord, I feel like that. Everyone around me shines so brightly for You, but I'm barely a twinkle."

A cloud passed over the star and it disappeared. "That's how I feel, God," I said. "Whenever a cloud of sadness comes over me, people can't see Your light in me at all. I want to shine for You every day of my life."

The cloud moved, and the star grew brighter until it was the brightest in that sky!

A few days later, I awoke filled with overwhelming joy. A stranger even said to me, "I can tell you love Jesus because it's all over your face!" God had answered my prayer and His joy has never left me since!

What was God's silent promise to me that night demonstrated through the stars? Read Daniel 9:3 and write what that means to you.

_____

_____

_____

As I shared my testimony, however, many adults I looked up to said, "God doesn't speak that way. He only speaks through the Bible."

Because I was so young and they were more experienced in their walk with God, I listened to them and closed the door on God's voice.

I wish I'd believed what God's Word says instead of man! It took 20 years for God to finally bust down the door, but He did.

Now *I listen to God, not man.*

"Behold, I stand at the door and knock. If anyone hears My voice and opens the door, I will come in to him and dine with him, and he with Me." Revelation 3:20

 12

Get in the Habit

of setting aside time in your quiet times to listen to God. Empty your mind and be still before Him. Psalm 46:10. Don't worry if you don't "hear" God's voice right away. Remember, He speaks in many ways all the time, even when your quiet time is over. Just keep your spiritual "ears" open and look out for His answers.

13 Chapter — DARE

to recognize God's voice

Want hearing aids?

Do you sometimes feel God is silent? Explain.

_____

_____

_____

Just because you can't hear God speaking doesn't mean He's not.

God speaks even through silence.

If you feel you can't hear the Lord, then that's a good time to ask Him if there is anything blocking your spiritual "ears."

Are you positioning yourself to listen? Are you reading the Word? Setting aside time to be still before Him? *Make sure you're not missing your quiet times and that you're allowing enough time for Him to speak.*

Is there unconfessed sin (like doubt, worry, pride, self-pity, unforgiveness, etc.) in the way? *Repent.*

Do you feel distracted in your quiet times? *Begin that time with prayer*, asking God to guard it and to guide it. Don't just stick to what you normally do. *Ask God what He wants to do and follow Him there.*

Do your thoughts dart about, making it difficult to focus? *Turn those thoughts into prayers, asking God what He wants for those situations and people.*

If you can't stop thinking about a task that needs to get done, like a phone call or something else you're

afraid you'll forget, *keep a notepad handy* so you can write that down, and then go back to listening.

Are you too stressed to quiet your heart? *Hand God whatever is troubling you.* Matthew 6:33. And *worship.*

Have you decided on the lie that God doesn't speak, or He speaks to others but not to you? ***If you expect God to speak, you're more likely to hear Him.***

Don't dismiss God's voice with, "That's just me" or "I'll think about that later." ***Tuning out God's voice is like closing the door in His face.***

What if you think you're hearing God but you're not sure? *Ask Him, "Lord, are you saying such-and-such?"* He might confirm it by highlighting a Scripture or sending you an encouraging phone call.

If you're still not sure, hand what You feel Him saying back over to Him: "Lord, it feels

like You're saying thus-and-so. I'm headed that way because I want to obey you. Please make Your will clear."

✐ The key to listening is obedience.

Each time you step out in faith to do what God asks of you, His voice gets louder and obeying Him gets easier.

But *if you ignore Him, there may come a time when you can no longer hear what He's saying.* Isaiah 55:6.

✐ If you really want to hear God's voice, *close the door to the other voices competing for your attention*. John 10:1-5.

The voice of my own **selfish desire** is usually the loudest. Jeremiah 17:9. I often get that one mixed up with God's because *I want it so badly I imagine He wants it too.* The only way to shut that door is to *give up my agendas* and be willing to do anything God wants. Sometimes what I want ends up being what He wants, but I have to surrender first to find out.

The voice of **doubt** says it's not God or that God doesn't speak. The voice of **reasoning** says, "That can't be right because...." The voice of **experience** decides what's right even before God speaks. The voices of **tradition** and **legalism** cover over God's voice with habits and rules. **Others**' voices can sway us, too, especially if we look up to those people.

Then there's my **enemy**. He likes to tell me what "sounds" true but is cunningly contrary to what God says. I have to be on the alert to notice. John 8:42-47, 2 Corinthians 10:3-5, 1 Peter 5:8, 1 Thessalonians 5:6.

So how can I know when God is speaking?

> **THREE-FOLD SIEVE FOR KNOWING GOD'S VOICE OF TRUTH:**
>
> 1. DOES IT LINE UP WITH THE WORD (ALL OF IT, NOT JUST ONE VERSE)?
> 2. DOES IT LINE UP WITH GOD'S CHARACTER (ESPECIALLY HIS LOVE AND GRACE)? MATTHEW 22:37-40.
> 3. DOES IT DRAW YOU (AND OTHERS) CLOSER TO HIM?

Take time today to ask God a question and listen for His answer. If you can't think of anything to ask, try asking Him what to ask. Whatever situation first pops into your thoughts, ask Him what He thinks about that and then write what you feel Him saying.

_____

_____

_____

Now run it through the Three-Fold Sieve. Does it line up with the Word (all of it)? How?

_____

_____

Does it line up with Love's character? How?

_____

_____

Does it draw you closer to God? How?

_____

_____

Take some time now to pray for that situation according to what you felt Him showing you and obey any instructions He gives you.

✐ 13 ✐

Get in the Habit

of not just doing whatever you feel like thinking or doing. Use the Three-fold Sieve to know which voice you're listening to. Ask God what He's doing, listen for His answer and join Him there. Isaiah 50:4-5.

A magnet for His majesty

What was different about Moses' relationship with God? See Numbers 12:6-8.

_____

_____

What was it about Moses that invited the Lord so near? See Numbers 12:3.

_____

_____

You can know the Word, obey God and seek to serve Him all your life, but without humility you'll miss out on the "more."

Humility draws us into God's presence and places us in the right position for intimacy with Him.

Wait! Moses _wrote_ Numbers. So he said of _himself_ he was "the humblest man in the world." How is _that_ humility?

God's definitions don't always match man's. _Humility is not disagreeing with someone who thinks well of you. It's not putting yourself down when you're really quite good at something._ Those are earthly definitions.

⌁ Humility is agreeing with God.

In other words, feeling like a failure is a form of pride, because God says you're "more than a conqueror." Romans 8:37.

Declining an invitation to preach on the basis of "I'm not good at that" is also pride, because Philippians 4:13 says you can do all things through Christ who strengthens you.

Of course, _if God tells you not to_ take that appointment, that's different. Then your decision isn't based on what you think about yourself or your fear of what others will think of you, but _on your desire to obey the Lord._

You can trust God's viewpoint. He knows you better than you know yourself.

In fact, one of my favorite questions to ask the Lord is, "When You look at me, what do You see?" He often shows me things I don't realize about myself and draws me back into His truth and purposes.

Take a moment to sit still before the Lord and ask Him that question. He may show you a picture, remind you of a verse or speak to you some other way. Run what you feel Him saying through the Three-Fold Sieve (Chapter 13) and write your experience here.

_____

_____

_____

_____

It's important to get in the habit of seeing things God's way, not only when you look at yourself but also when you look at others.

Pride says, "I'm better than you." It looks down on people for not being or doing what you think is best.

But humility sees others with Heaven's eyes. _**Get in the habit of laying all your opinions at Jesus' feet and asking Him for His.**_

In fact, let's do that right now. Is there someone who rubs you the wrong way? Surrender your opinions of that person over to the Lord. (You can write in your journal.)

Now ask God how _He_ sees that person. He may show you what they're going through or speak a verse over them or tell you of His plans for their lives. Write in your journal what you feel Him saying and run it through the Sieve to make sure it's God speaking and not your own judgments or someone else's.

How do you feel about that person now?

_____

_____

An enemy lie may seem "true" in an earthly sense, but if it makes us worried or angry or leads us down opposite paths from love and grace, then it's probably not God's viewpoint. Matthew 22:37-40, Galatians 5:22.

Just because I believe something doesn't make it true. Only what God says is true. When I disagree with Him, I set myself above Him, *as if I know better than God.*

Disagreeing with God is not only proud, it is dangerous. John 8:42-47, Isaiah 30:9-15, James 4:6. God is holy, righteous, omnipotent, omniscient, omnipresent, and your Creator. Nothing is hidden from Him. When He shows you something, especially if it's sin, listen up.

The easiest way to break free from a sin stronghold is to see your sin the way God sees it, to *agree with Him* about it.

Let that sin become so repulsive to you, as you sit in the presence of the Holy One you love, that you *never want to do it again.*

 **Humility is surrendering to God.**

What does 2 Corinthians 10:3-5 say we should do with our thoughts? Why is that important? See Isaiah 55:6-9. _____

_____

_____

So how do you know what God's thoughts are? *By walking close to Him, taking time to listen to His heart in your quiet times, reading the Word, laying down your opinions and ideas at His feet and asking Him for His.*

When we humble ourselves before God, surrendering our ways to His Sovereignty, we become one with Him, just as Jesus was one with His Father. John 14:14-21.

What does John 5:19 say about Jesus? How is that a good example for us to follow too? Proverbs 3:5-7. _____

_____

_____

 **Humility is depending on God.**

A few years ago, I felt God urging me to teach a Bible study, but whenever I specifically asked Him if He wanted me to, I heard Him say no. Confused, I asked Him again, *"Do You want me to teach that Bible study this fall?"*

"No!" His voice resounded in my heart and mind. *"I want to teach it."*

I had asked the wrong question!

So, I rephrased it. "Do You want me to be a warm body in the room while *YOU* teach?"

"YES!" came the emphatic reply.

That Bible study turned out to be one of the most unforgettable experiences of my life. Every time we got together, God performed miracles and radically transformed us. I'm so glad I let Him teach!

 **Humility is focusing your eyes on God, not yourself.**

If God is your everything, the One you live for, then there's no room to spend your thoughts on how incapable you are, because He makes all things possible! Luke 1:37.

 **Humility is always being conscious you are in the presence of One greater than you.**

— 14 —

Get in the Habit

... of surrendering all your thoughts and opinions over to God and asking Him for His so you can agree with Him. Submit to His ways, remembering that you are always in the presence of One greater than you.

DARE

to fear the Lord

No more "eye-dulls"

The words "fear" and "afraid" appear hundreds of times in the Word, but nearly every verse says one of two things: *"Fear not"* or *"Fear the Lord."*

So why are we afraid of what others think of us, of messing up, of being left out, of what might happen to us, or of whatever else it is that keeps our minds busy with worry?

It's an eyes issue. *What are you looking at?* Are you looking at what you expect to happen or to God who can do anything? Are you looking at your needs or to your Provider? Are you relying on your own abilities or His power? Are you looking to man for approval or to God? Galatians 1:10.

If your eyes are on God and you walk in the confidence that your times are in His hands (Psalm 31:15), *you will be a man of rest, peace and confidence, not a man of fear.* 2 Timothy 1:7. **Then *He* will be the One you "fear," not people or circumstances.**

I guess you could say, *anything else you focus on can become an "eye-dull."*

Taking your focus off God and bowing to fear, self-pity, pride, etc., blocks your view of how all-powerful and loving God is.

Besides that, *idols make Him jealous.* Exodus 20:3-5. He's likely to **cast down your eye-dull!**

And that's a good thing. You want Him to break the chains of fear of man (or whatever else attracts your attention), and set you free to love, adore and *fear* only Him.

If you submit to God's discipline, you will find freedom, joy and the power to walk in victory. Hebrews 12:7-13.

When I was sick with an incurable disease that promised to leave me blind, insane, in terrible pain and bed-ridden for the rest of my life, I cried out, "But, Lord, I never thought my life would turn out this way! I wanted to be a great mom and wife....

"WHOSE life?" God interrupted me.

"Oh, yeah. Uh, *Yours*, Lord. I gave my life to *You*." Somehow in my self-pity I'd forgotten.

That was a definite fear-of-the-Lord experience for me. As I surrendered my thoughts, desires, dreams, *everything* to Him (2 Corinthians 10:5) throughout the next few months, trusting in His goodness, even if His plans were different from mine, *He healed me.*

He didn't have to. He had already filled me with joy and peace no matter what happened. But *perhaps surrender was what He was waiting for.* After all, oneness with Him is His first will for my life, and **there's no faster way to oneness than surrender.**

What about you? Have you ever experienced fear of the Lord? Explain.

_____

_____

_____

So what does it mean to fear the Lord? The word in Hebrew holds the idea of awe, piety, reverence. But its main meaning is fear, terror.

Don't be mistaken, God is not to be trifled with. Check out Deuteronomy 28. The first 14 verses of blessings for those who worship and obey the Lord are followed by 54 verses of curses that fall on those who don't. And He is still a God to be feared in the New Testament, as well. See Acts 5:1-11.

Galatians 5:16-21 says that those who are selfish, argumentative, impure, angry, and participate in cliques, among other things, "will not inherit the kingdom of God."

That's a scary list a lot of "Christians" are on. *None of those things are worth forfeiting your inheritance.*

Are you on that list? Pray through it together with God and ask Him. Write what comes to mind and repent as He leads.

_____
_____
_____
_____

According to Exodus 20:20, what is the purpose of fear of the Lord?

_____
_____
_____

When you live a life of awe and reverence for the Lord, you're more afraid of the consequences of *not* obeying God than you are of not getting what you want.

In fact, *when you love the Lord with all your heart, what He wants is all you want* because **you rest in His love** and **trust in His Sovereignty**. Isaiah 30:15.

Most fears drive you away or make you want to protect yourself from what you're afraid of. But running from God because you're afraid of what He'll ask you to do or what you think He'll tell you not to do is not true fear of the Lord. It's simply *rebellion*.

When you run from Jesus, what do you miss out on? John 10:10. And what might the enemy steal from you? Or destroy? How could giving in to temptation kill the abundant, joy-filled life that's yours in Christ?

_____
_____

Fear of the Lord is not like earthly fears. It is a safe fear that draws us near and deepens our faith. It leads us to repentance, restores us to the One we love and sets our feet back on the right path to joy, peace and the power of His Spirit flowing through us.

*When you fear the Lord, you love Him and trust in His goodness and love so completely you wouldn't **dare** step off His paths for fear of **missing His presence.***

What do Proverbs 9:10, 10:27, 14:27, 8:13 and 19:23 say about fear of the Lord?

_____
_____
_____

"The fear of the Lord is the beginning of wisdom." Psalm 111:10

15

Get in the Habit
of fearing God and trusting Him so deeply you wouldn't dare step off His paths for fear of missing out on His blessings and miracles.

to lay down your idols

The root of the problem

God is gentle, abounding in love, and slow to get angry. But He is also just, holy and **worthy of obedience**. Romans 6, Deuteronomy 11.

The truth is many believers don't walk in enough **fear of the Lord** or **passion for Him** to obey Him on a constant basis. Proverbs 1:7.

Read 1 Samuel 15. Is partial obedience still obedience? _____

Why did Saul disobey God? Whom was he afraid of? v. 24. _____

Fear of man brings a snare, but whoever trusts in the LORD shall be safe." Proverbs 29:25

Fear of man is one of the main idols we tend to worship over God.

We're afraid of what someone will say or do or think — usually about us. And that is what drives our decision-making instead of God's Word and His Spirit.

Have you ever felt the urge to raise your hands in worship at church, but didn't because you were afraid others might see you?

Have you ever wanted to talk about Jesus with your friends, but didn't because you were afraid of what they might think?

Have you ever done something you know is wrong because you were afraid of how your friends would treat you if you didn't?

Has God ever told you to confront someone on sin, but you didn't because you were afraid of their response?

Think back on the past few weeks. Is there any way fear has kept you from obedience?

_____
_____
_____

In Chapter 11, I told you my leaders forbid me to speak of "trembling" in God's manifest presence. How is that contrary to Nahum 1:5, Proverbs 28:14 and Acts 7:32?

_____
_____
_____

None of my accusers came to me directly, but the man they sent to deal with me told me they were afraid the donors would stop giving to the organization. In other words, they were afraid of losing money and apparently afraid of me. But did they fear the Lord?

Don't let others' fears dissuade you. Know the Word, know God's character, and fear Him alone. Isaiah 8:12-14a.

If Satan's aim is to keep us from oneness with Christ, then if we're not listening to God, whom are we obeying? _____.
That's why 1 Samuel 15:23 compares *rebellion* to _____.

What does that verse compare pride to? _____. Whom did Saul "worship" at Gilgal? 1 Samuel 15:12.

_____

God is no burglar out to steal your good time. If you choose to go against His purposes, then you are choosing the enemy's plans for your life. And that is *dangerous*.

What does Isaiah 2:11 say? Why? What is God's attitude toward pride? 1 Peter 5:5.

_____
_____
_____

And what is His attitude toward humility? James 4:6, 10. _____

In Proverbs 11:2, with pride comes _____, but with humility comes _____.

🖛 Pride separates us from God.

It's kind of like trying to find Him through a mountain of self. He's talking, but you're so focused on your own stuff you can't hear Him.

What are some of pride's qualities in Psalm 10:4, 31:18, Proverbs 14:3, Philippians 2:1-16?

_____
_____
_____
_____
_____

Self-pity is a form of pride because you're focused on what you want that you didn't get.

Judgment is a form of pride because you're focused on someone else's sin, rather than cleaning out your own heart. Matthew 7:1-5.

Looking down on yourself is a form of pride because your thoughts are all about you, rather than God.

Selfishness and **laziness** are forms of pride because you're doing what you want instead of loving and serving God and others.

What other forms of pride can you think of? _____
_____
_____

Proverbs 13:10 tells us wherever there is disagreement or strife, ***you can be sure pride is at the heart of it.***

Is there anyone you've had a disagreement with? What part did pride play in your thoughts and reactions? Matthew 7:1-5. Ask God and write what He brings to mind.

_____
_____

In what ways has your pride or fear of man separated you from God? What other idols do you need to lay down before the Lord? Ask Him and write what comes to mind.

_____
_____
_____

Meditate on 1 Samuel 5:1-5. The ark was a symbol of God's presence. What happened when it was brought into Dagon's temple?

_____
_____
_____

Spend some time in worship, focusing on God's holiness and glory. Picture bringing each one of your idols into His holy presence and watching them crumble at His feet. Bow before Him acknowledging that He alone is Lord of your life. Write your prayer of repentance and commitment.

_____
_____
_____
_____
_____

As you walk out into the world this week, let the Lord show you when your thoughts turn away from Him. Watch for the lies that lead you back to your idols and make conscious decisions to stand on God's truth, fearing and obeying Him alone.

🖛 16 🖛

Get in the Habit

of worshipping and obeying God alone, not pride, fear of man or any other idol. If you're not sure what God wants you to do, choose the path that loves Him and others. Matthew 22:37-40, Romans 13:8-10, 1 John 4:18.

Chapter 17

to obey the King of Kings

Advantage to win

Can you think of a time when you obeyed the Lord and were glad you did? Explain.

_____

_____

_____

Obeying God is not merely adhering to a list of dos and don'ts expected of you. Ephesians 2:8-9. That would be *legalism*, an enemy stronghold that sucks the life out of you and those around you because *it makes Christianity about doing what is expected of you; rather than enjoying Christ. It makes walking His paths a burden, not a joy.*

True obedience flows naturally from a passionate love for Christ.

➤ The closer you walk with Jesus, the easier it is to obey Him.

John 14:15 says to my heart: "If you really love Me, you will have no problem obeying Me because it will be all you want to do!"

Matthew 22:37-40 joins that verse to do away with long lists of dos and don'ts because **love is our one command.** *If you're loving God and loving others, then you're doing everything your King asks of you.*

Read James 1:22-25. What does the cartoon at right mean to you? Matthew 21:28-32.

_____

_____

_____

➤ Obedience to Christ is to your advantage. 1 John 5:3-5, Deuteronomy 29:13.

You don't want to miss out. This God Who loves you and created you knows much better than you do what is best for your life. If you head off in your own directions now, driven by what you or other people want, by the time you realize what a mistake you've made, *it may be too late.* Jeremiah 29:11, Isaiah 55:6-9, Matthew 7:24-27.

God can bring something good out of your wrong choices and messy relationships. But *you really don't want to miss the blessing of a life surrendered to your King.*

What if that beautiful woman of God He prepared for you passes you by because you're too busy fitting in with the boys and kissing the wrong girls to shine like the man of God she's looking for?

I can't begin to imagine what my life would be like if I hadn't chosen early on to follow Christ. I would have missed out on so many wonderful adventures with my man-of-God husband taking Christ's light into dark corners of the world. In fact, I might not even have married him at all! Then we wouldn't have these amazing children or all those exciting experiences together.

The choices you make now have everything to do with how the rest of your life goes.

➤ Our rewards may not be what we hope, but *God most definitely rewards us with more of Himself when we obey.*

The more you obey the Lord, the closer you get to Him. The closer you get to Him, the louder His voice is and the easier it is to obey. It's a joyous cycle of peace and victory.

➤ Obedience to Christ positions us to overcome. Romans 8:28-37.

Not that life is always smooth sailing when we obey. Sometimes obedience costs and surrender can be painful. Whether we follow

God or not, we will face difficulties in life. **The difference for the one who chooses God's path through the trials is that *He walks it with us*.** Matthew 28:20.

*"I have told you these things, so that in Me you may have peace. In this world you will have trouble. But take heart! **I have overcome the world.**"* John 16:33 (NIV)

🐾 **There is joy in obedience, no matter how many people oppose you or how difficult your circumstances are.** Acts 13:49-52.

Losing friends or a job or anything else for the sake of the Lord is never fun. But really, the friends I want around me are those who encourage me to walk in God's ways, not in sin. And if I lose my job, then it's worth it for

the joy of His felt presence. 1 Peter 4:12-19.

What do you have to lose if you obey Christ? Read Joshua 24:14-16 and write a prayer of commitment.

_____
_____
_____
_____
_____

Is there anything God has asked you to do that you haven't done yet? Is there anything He has asked you *not* to do that you're still doing? What's keeping you from obedience?

_____
_____
_____
_____

 17 〰️

Get in the Habit

of looking for your King's commands each day as you read the Word—like "Fear not," "Praise the Lord," "Be still and know that I am God," etc. Ask God to help you walk out in His Word through life's experiences.

Chapter 18

DARE

to make wise decisions

What are you leaning on?

How do you normally make big decisions?

_____
_____
_____

What about small decisions, like whether or not to go out with your friends or which TV show to watch or when to wash dishes?

_____
_____
_____

Mark the following that apply: Have you ever made decisions based on
__ what you think is best?
__ what you want?
__ fear of what might happen?
__ fear of what others will think?
__ pressure from people?
__ time constraints?
__ others' advice?
__ experience?
__ need?
__ accomplishment, ambition?
__ other _____?

Usually our method for making decisions depends on importance or urgency. We might make up a list of pros and cons for big decisions, ask others for advice, even pray, especially if we're not sure what to do. But for more day-to-day decisions, we probably just lean on our own understanding. Is that true for you? Explain.

_____
_____
_____

In Proverbs 3:5-6, which decisions are we to seek God for? _____
And when should we lean on our own un-

derstanding? _____

When did Jesus do the will of His Father? John 8:29b. _____

One Christian leader I worked under based most of his decisions on fear (of what others will think, of losing his job, of what he thinks someone will do, of what might happen, etc.). How is faith opposite to fear? Deuteronomy 31:8, Hebrews 13:6. _____
_____

How did Jesus make decisions? Luke 6:13-16. _____
_____

That same leader argued some decisions must be made fast; no time to pray. _But it only takes one second to pray, "Show me what to do, Lord."_ **One second of surrender can make the whole difference, even win the battle.**

Another Christian leader who boasted he had the gift of wisdom based most of his decisions on mind-reads. If facts didn't agree with what he assumed, or people didn't say what he thought they would, he relied on his own imaginations rather than the truth.

Did he truly have the gift of wisdom? Why or why not? John 8:31-32, 42-47, 14:6.

_____

The spiritual gift of wisdom flows from God's empowering as we listen to Him and walk in obedience to His Spirit's leadership.

A wise man knows he can't lean on his own understanding, even if he has all the "facts," because _man's wisdom isn't complete._

"'My thoughts are not your thoughts, nor are your ways My ways,' says the Lord. 'For as the **_heavens are higher than the earth, so are_**

My ways higher than your ways, and My thoughts than your thoughts.'" Isaiah 55:8-9

When God looks for someone to do great things for Him, He most often chooses those who love Him and are surrendered to His purposes. John 14:15.

If you have chosen Christ as your King, then no matter how incapable you feel to do the things He calls you to do, know this: **Wisdom Himself lives within you.** 1 Corinthians 1:26-30. So *lean on Him.*

How to make wise decisions:

1. Before you react, before you worry, before you go to someone else for advice or help, *pray. Ask God what He wants to do. Listen for His answer.*

2. Make sure you *know the facts.* Do some research. Talk to people who are in the situation and know it well. Watch the news. Know what the Word says about it.

3. Be willing to be wrong. Your way is not the only way, and may not even be the best way. *Lay your agendas down and ask God for His.* Isaiah 55:8.

4. Take time to *listen.* What is God saying to those who will be affected by your decision? What experience does someone close to the Lord have in that area? *Pray together* with them for His will.

5. Run others' advice through the Three-Fold Sieve (Chapter 13) and *only receive what GOD is saying.* James 4:11-12.

6. What do you feel God leading you to do? Do you feel a peace about that? *Make sure everything you do agrees with Love.* Matthew 22:37-40.

7. Then *hand your decision to God again.* "Lord, it feels like You're saying..., so I'm headed in that direction to follow You. Show me clearly if I'm wrong."

Obviously, that method can't be done in a second. But if you get in the habit of making wise decisions by seeking God, then you will naturally flow in His Spirit, and when the pressure's on you will know what God is doing and follow Him there immediately.

It takes a lifestyle change to walk in the Spirit.

Let's try the above method now. What decision are you facing? Write it out to God here.

_____

_____

What are the facts? What are others saying to you? What are your own opinions and ideas on the matter? Hand those over to the Lord.

_____

_____

Who will be affected by your decision? Who has wisdom in the area? Seek God's will together in prayer with them. Listen to what God's showing them and lay that before Him.

_____

_____

Ask God what He wants to do. Hand what you feel Him saying back to Him.

_____

_____

Whatever God asks you to do will always agree with Matthew 22:37-40. Why?

_____

_____

18

Get in the Habit

of asking God what He's doing and joining Him there. Don't wait for the big decisions, though. Ask Him what He wants to do all throughout the day, no matter how small the decision is. Get in the habit of surrendering and listening to Him. Then you will naturally follow His lead.

❧ Part 3 ❧

"Be strong in the Lord and in the power of His might. Put on the whole armor of God, that you may be able to stand against the wiles of the devil. For we do not wrestle against flesh and blood, but against principalities, against powers, against the rulers of the darkness of this age, against spiritual hosts of wickedness in the heavenly places. Therefore take up the whole armor of God, that you may be able to withstand in the evil day, and having done all, to stand."

Ephesians 6:10-13

At War

Chapter 19

DARE
to armor up

Don't get caught naked!

Imagine attending a fashion show for the latest styles for Godly men. According to Colossians 3:5-14, what clothes are "out"?

_____

_____

_____

What clothes are "in" Godly fashion?

_____

_____

In the spiritual realm, the clothing you wear defines who you are.

Why? What does Romans 13:14 say we should clothe ourselves with?

_____

How does that make us different from the world? _____

_____

A believer clothed in humility (1 Peter 5:5) and wearing all his spiritual armor (Ephesians 6:10-18) is less likely to be ripped up by our enemy, the "roaring lion" (1 Peter 5:8), than a rebellious man (Isaiah 1:5-6) who left all his clothing and armor at home.

"Be strong in the Lord and in the power of His might. Put on the whole armor of God, that you may be able to stand against the wiles of the devil. For we do not wrestle against flesh and blood, but against principalities, against powers, against the rulers of the darkness of this age, against spiritual hosts of wickedness in the heavenly places. Therefore take up the whole armor of God, that you may be able to withstand in the evil day, and having done all, to stand. Stand therefore, having girded your waist with truth, having put on the breastplate of righteousness, and having shod your feet with the preparation of the Gospel of peace; above all, taking the shield of faith with which you will be able to quench all the fiery darts of the wicked one. And take the helmet of salvation, and the sword of the Spirit, which is the Word of God; praying always with all prayer and supplication in the Spirit, being watchful to this end with all perseverance." Ephesians 6:10-18

In ancient Roman days, the **belt** bound up a soldier's robes so the folds wouldn't get in the way and hinder his movement. Lies (John 8:43-47) can hinder us from walking in the **truth** of who we are in Christ, tripping us up and making us fall, rather than setting us *free* (John 8:31-32) *to move in Him.*

Proverbs 4:23 advises us to *guard our heart* "above all." When the enemy attacks the things closest to our hearts (Matthew 6:21), it is the **breastplate of righteousness** that protects us—the fullness of what Christ has done for us—not our own righteous acts.

The **readiness that comes from the Gospel of peace** should be on our feet at all times. These combat boots *walk us into the war zones of dissensions and arguments, difficulties and trials; bringing peace* that comes from a prayerful and thankful heart (Philippians 4:4-7) and the good news that Jesus is the answer. What does Isaiah 52:7 say about our feet when they're shod this way?

_____

The **shield of faith** *puts out the fire of the enemy* (Ephesians 6:16), and can also be used as a *ramming wall to knock the enemy down.*

The **helmet of salvation** *protects our mind from enemy attacks* through our thoughts.

And the **sword of the Spirit, the Word of**

God, is our *offensive weapon to defeat the enemy.* So know it well. 2 Timothy 3:16-17.

In the spiritual realm, **our armor is not just a metaphor. It is REAL.** The enemy can see where we're vulnerable, and that is where he will strike.

*"Put on the armor of light… Clothe yourselves with the Lord Jesus Christ… Because **when we are clothed, we will not be found naked.**"*
Romans 13:12-14; 2 Corinthians 5:3

Look over the list of clothing and armor (Colossians 3:12-14 and Ephesians 6:10-18). What are you already wearing well? When others look at you, what do they see?

What do you need to put on more of?

Pull out your "sword" and ask God to show you a verse to memorize that you will need for a future "battle." Write it here and then be on the ready in days to come.

～ 19 ～

Get in the Habit

of putting on your armor every day. The enemy can see when you've dropped your armor, and he will attack you in those exposed places. But most of all, be clothed with Christ. The closer you walk with Him, the more you take on His qualities. And the more you look like Him, the more your enemy trembles. Romans 8:35-39.

Chapter 20 — DARE

to fight for the things that matter

To fight or not to fight

What do we fight for? See Psalm 45:3-7; 1 Timothy 1:18-19; 6:11-12.

_____

_____

What is the prize? See 2 Timothy 4:7-8.

_____

One day, as I helped out at a church event, the woman in charge took a task from her daughter and handed it to me. Not wanting the teen to feel hurt, I praised her for her giftings in other areas where I'm lacking.

Afterwards, her father marched up to me screaming, "You should have given her that task! How dare you! Apologize to her for the mean things you said!"

Mean things? You can imagine what I was thinking. It went something like, "I was just following your wife's orders. *She's* the one you should be yelling at. I was being *nice!*"

But as fast as I could, I dumped those thoughts into Jesus' lap, and then said, "What time can I come by today to apologize?"

I knew I needed to fight for the things that matter, and my pride isn't one of those things! A wounded teenager is.

I'll admit, I was scared—not of the sweet daughter, but of her Doberman dad. It's my experience that angry people just get angrier when you apologize; I feared facing a monster!

So I got on my face before the Lord, laid down all my thoughts and opinions at Jesus' feet and asked Him for His. He showed me how beloved this young woman is to Him and how she was willing to do the things no one else would for Him.

By the time I got to her home, I was so honored to be in the presence of one He loved so much I knelt at her feet to ask forgiveness. Then I told her what God had said about her. Sweet tears slid down her cheeks as His love washed over her.

But my task wasn't over. I felt the Lord say, "Now I want to speak to the father."

My heart raged, "Sure! I'll give him a piece of Your mind for You! That guy's got serious anger issues!"

But when I opened my mouth, the Holy Spirit that flowed out surprised me. I found myself saying, "God wants you to know He saw what happened when you were a child. Now you have become a defender of the little ones, and He stands beside you."

Now, *that was a turn of events I never saw coming!*

You have an enemy, but it's not your brother. So fight *for* your brother, not against him.
Ephesians 6:12.

The battle isn't to prove you're right, or to get your brother to agree with you, or to make him do what you want, but *to expose Satan's schemes so God can set you both free.* 2 Corinthians 10:3-5.

Your weapons in this battle between light and darkness are not of this world. Wear your armor (Ephesians 6:14) and wield the Word of God (Ephesians 6:17). Remember that ***it is in prayer that the battle is won.*** Ephesians 6:18.

Notice how I prayed and God changed my heart *before* I engaged in battle. That way, I could **come in line with what God was doing, rather than what the enemy was doing.**

What was the enemy doing in that conflict?

_____

What did God do? _____

When Jesus turned over the tables at the temple (Mark 11:15-17), He didn't do it on a whim or in uncontrolled rage. He looked around the day before (Mark 11:11) and *waited until the next day to act on what he saw.*

Likewise, it's good for you not to lash out immediately when you're angry. Rather, **take time to get with the Lord and let your thoughts come in line with His.** Isaiah 55:6-9. Check your own heart out and make sure the sin isn't actually yours. Matthew 7:1-5.

Then when you finally approach others about their sin, as in Matthew 18:15, you will do it with a *humble heart, speaking the truth in love* (Ephesians 4:15), and with the purpose of *fighting for their freedom.*

Don't worry if you mess up. Everyone misunderstands sometimes or says things he shouldn't. But when that happens, **be quick to ask forgiveness** of the person you hurt.

And get with the Lord. **Let Him clean out your heart.** He may want to set you free from a sin or wrong thought process and this very event may be how He exposes it. (Chapter 22.)

Choose your battles well. How to squeeze the toothpaste or whether the top is put back on aren't issues worth getting angry about. Likewise, opinions or politics or sports or anything else—if they aren't eternal issues founded in the Word, they aren't worth losing friendships over. James 4:1-3.

Are you in a conflict right now? Try these steps to resolution and peace in conflict:

1. Be **quick to listen, slow to speak, and slow to get angry.** James 1:19.

2. Don't just react. Lay down your thoughts and **ask God for His.** Mark 11:11-17; Proverbs 3:5-7; Isaiah 55:6-9. Get alone as soon as you can and pray. Use the Galatians 5:22-23 Gauge in Chapter 22.

3. **Check for sin**. Did you have a part in the conflict? Matthew 7:1-5.

4. If so, **ask forgiveness.** 1 John 1:8-10.

5. NO MIND-READING. Make sure you **know the facts before you accuse.** Ask, "When you said…, did you mean…?" Only God knows what your brother's thinking and only He is the Judge of his motives. James 4:11-12. *You want to be on the side of* **Love** *(1 John 4:16) and* **Truth** *(John 14:6), not the Accuser (Revelation 12:10) and Father of Lies (John 8:44).*

6. Choose to **do the opposite of what the enemy is doing**. Is he making you angry? *Forgive.* Is he causing division? *Love.* Is he discouraging you? *Worship.* Is he manipulating you? *Do what God wants.*

7. Pray and **ask God what He's doing**, so you can come in line with His purposes. Is he asking you to let Him fight for you? Exodus 14:14. To step out and love those fighting against you? Romans 12. **Whatever He's doing, He is most certainly drawing you closer to Himself.** So lean into Him through this trial—tell Him how you feel, listen for His voice, let Him guide you. Exodus 33:14; 23:20-22; 9:16; Isaiah 42:13; 58:8-9.

8. **Forgive.** Mark 11:25. (Chapter 37)

❧ 20 ❧

Get in the Habit

of checking your own heart out first before you point your finger at someone else. Let God show you why you feel or react the way you do so He can replace any lies with His truth and change you. You can't change someone else, but when you change, others often change too.

Chapter 21

DARE

to defy enemy schemes

Double agent? No!

What if you were a secret service agent and the enemy came up to you and said, "Why don't you double cross your partner?"

You'd say, "No way!"

But what if he disguises himself and defends you in a jam. You start to trust him. Then he makes subtle comments here and there to suggest your partner is a double agent. You begin to notice things he does that make you believe it might be true.

At last, with your conscience clear that you're protecting your country, you join with the enemy agent, sabotage one of your partner's missions, and turn him in as a traitor. *Now* who's the double agent?

Did you set out to work for the enemy? No, of course not. But you gave in to his schemes.

You have a real enemy—Satan—who is out to destroy those who follow God. And *he most often uses God's own people to do it.* He is so sneaky about it, in fact, that **they think they are obeying God!**

How many churches have split, each side thinking they were right in their stand against the other? How many Christian relationships have broken apart? How many marriages?

If you're on the alert, you might be able to discern when the enemy's attacking and even what he's doing: he's discouraging you, dividing a friendship, wanting you to wallow in self-pity, trying to make you lose your temper, keeping you from doing what God wants….

But *no matter what the enemy is doing, God is doing so much more.*

In fact, *God is so sovereign that even the enemy is subject to Him.* That means

Satan can't attack you unless God allows it.

And if God allows it, then it is because He is doing something good in you.

One time, I remember God urging me to apologize to my husband for something. His reaction was so defensive that I asked him, "What do you think I just said?"

The sentence he quoted back to me *rhymed with my sentence word for word,* but it was an *accusation,* not an apology. *The enemy had twisted my words in the air!*

Rather than arguing like the enemy had intended, we prayed together. We fought against misunderstanding and dissension, and learned ways to guard against further attacks. We grew closer to each other and closer to the Lord, and have taught other couples the things we've learned. So, **what the enemy meant for evil, God used for good.**

Don't miss out on the hidden treasures and eternal rewards God has prepared for you in every trial. *Find out what God's doing and join Him there!*

If you're not sure what He's doing, at least **purpose to do the opposite of what the enemy is doing.**

For instance, instead of complaining, *thank God.* If you're depressed, *worship.* If you're angry at someone, *pray for him and bless him.* Romans 12:14, 17-21, Philippians 2:14-16.

What does Proverbs 3:5-7 say to you?

_____

_____

_____

Surrender to God is your key to winning every battle.

Don't just say, "God must be teaching me patience (or whatever)," and then resume your old ways when the trial is done.

If the battle doesn't change you, you will find yourself on the same battlefront over and over again until you "get it."

God loves you enough to do whatever it takes to knock down the idols and strongholds that keep you from walking in the Spirit.

It takes the friction of scrubbing against the grain of the fabric of who you used to be to release those stubborn stains and make you the person God created you to be.

And friction can be very uncomfortable.

It may feel easier to lose your temper and say, "That's just how I am."

But once you can clearly see how the enemy uses you when you're angry and what it does to your heart and to those around you, you might opt out of the double-agent deal and let God set you free from that battle altogether.

It's true. Once God sets you free, the enemy eventually stops pressing that old trigger in you because *he loses ground when all that comes out of you is Jesus.*

Oh, he'll find other ways to wage war against you and you'll live to fight another day. But *if you get in the habit of opposing the enemy by surrendering to what God is doing in every battle, Satan will never win a fight and you'll pile up a lot of treasure!*

And don't underestimate what God might be doing in the hearts of the people around you through your trial. What if someone comes to the Lord through your loving reactions or draws closer to Him?

Doing what God is doing brings forth eternal results.

What difficulties are you facing?

What does it seem the enemy could be doing in those circumstances?

How can you do the opposite?

Ask God, "What are You doing? How can I join you there?" Write what comes to mind.

Again, don't worry if you can't hear His answer straight away. The important thing is to ask Him and to leave your heart open before Him. Be sure and check for any sin or lies that might be blocking you from hearing His voice. *If you walk close to Him, trusting Him to answer you and guide you, then you won't miss what He's doing.*

He's usually doing many things, so don't stop at just one answer. Most specifically, ask Him what He's doing *in your heart.* Is there any attitude, sin, or thought process in you that's been exposed through this trial that the Lord might want to set you free from? Ask Him where that attitude or sin comes from, let Him show you the lies, and then His truth.

Don't waste this trial. Surrender to the Lord and His purposes. Let Him change you and set you free from the things within you that made the trial so difficult. Then next time a similar trial comes, you will soar over it on His wings of freedom.

⟳ 21 ⟲

Get in the Habit
of doing the opposite of what the enemy is doing in every circumstance. Look for what God is doing, and do that instead.

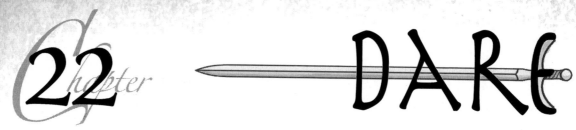

Chapter 22

DARE

to know the truth and live it

Get out of that prison!

If you knew you were trapped in a dungeon, wouldn't you want to be free?

Most believers who are captives don't even realize it. They live and die thinking the thought trap or sin pit they're in is "normal."

"This is just the way I am," they say. " "Everyone deals with that. "This is the cross I have to bear." "God made me this way."

No! God did *not* make you for lust or depression or rage or impatience or rejection or anything else outside the fruit of the Spirit.

He made you for love, joy and peace, **to walk in His Spirit as one with Him, shining so brightly with His love that you draw others into Him too.** Galatians 5:22-23, John 5:19, John 14-17. *He made you for freedom.* 2 Corinthians 3:17.

In Him, you are a *new* creation. 2 Corinthians 5:17. You may still feel confined by some of those old sin patterns and wrong thought processes, but *that is not who you are.*

Give the Spirit of Truth a few minutes of your quiet time to lay some strategic dynamite around those old lies that form your prison walls and kaboom! *That jail is a bust!*

Spiritually speaking, a "lie" is anything that is contrary to what God says.

In John 8:42-47, Jesus explained how the father of lies works. From the time we are young, he speaks the same old lies over and over until his language is so familiar to us that the truth Jesus speaks is hard to believe.

Let's say you make a mistake as a child. "You can't do anything right!" your father says. Then you mess up on a project for school and your teacher is disappointed. "I can't do anything right," you think. Sure enough, every assignment, every relationship, every job the rest of your life—*you just can't seem to ever get it right.*

In other words, the enemy used, "You can't do anything right," to build a stronghold of failure, reinforcing the lie-walls with experiences to prove you really are a failure.

But what does Philippians 4:13 say?

_____

_____

_____

You may know that verse in your head, but until **the truth you know becomes the truth you live,** it's just a happy sentence.

Christ has already won the victory. 1 Corinthians 15:55-57. But *He also calls us to fight against the enemy and win through His power.* 1 Timothy 6:12, Ephesians 6:10-18, 2 Corinthians 10:3-5, 1 Thessalonians 5:8.

How lies can get a hold on us:

1. The enemy usually **introduces a lie** to us through *negative life experiences.*

2. Believing and *acting on the lie* (sinning) gives him a **foothold.** Ephesians 4:27.

3. Now that he is *invited* (you opened the door by agreeing with him rather than God in that matter) he **fortifies the lie** with more lies (and more negative life experiences to make those lies sound "true") and builds a **stronghold.**

4. Built by lies that set themselves up against the knowledge of God, **strongholds lead us** to act and *react contrary to the Spirit.* 2 Corinthians 10:3-5, Romans 7:14-25.

So how do you know you're believing a lie? And how do you position yourself for the One Whose name is Truth to knock it down?

Use the Galatians 5:22-23 Gauge.

Memorize the fruit of the Spirit:

- _____
- _____
- _____
- _____
- _____
- _____
- _____
- _____
- _____

1. Notice when you feel angry, afraid, discontent or anything else negative outside the fruit of the Spirit.

2. As soon as you can, excuse yourself from the situation and get alone with God.

3. Ask Him why you feel that way. Don't just say, "I'm mad because he said thus-and-so!" _Don't look at what others did wrong; look at what's going on in your own heart._

4. Ask God where that feeling, thought or reaction first came in. Let Him take you anywhere He wants to take you and show you anything He wants to show you.

5. If He brings a memory to mind, remember what you felt when that happened. Look for the lies, like "No one cares," or "I'm not good enough," or "I have to defend myself," etc. Also, look for vows like, "I'll never let anyone do that to me again!"

6. Now ask God for His truth. He was there when that happened. Ask Him what He was saying and doing.

7. He might remind you of a verse, speak loving words to you, or show you what He was doing when that happened. _This is His truth that demolishes the lie, so listen up._ Run what you feel Him saying through the Three-Fold Sieve (Chapter 13).

Do a Word Search.

Look up in a concordance (there are free ones online) **all the verses that have to do with your issue.**

For example, if you struggle with fear, look up all the verses with the words "fear" or "afraid," and the opposites, "faith" or "trust."

Keep a journal of what God's showing you through His Word.

Walking in the truth will not only mean freedom from the control of lies, but also greater intimacy with Christ, which is what you were created for.

Get in the habit of checking your thoughts: What were you thinking when you did that? Were you being selfish ("I need that!")? Were you pushing an agenda that God hasn't asked you to push ("They should do it my way!")? Were you judging ("He really should…")?

Know what the Word says and **live it**. Through everything in life, don't lean on your own understanding, but seek the Lord. **Find out what He says about it; then live that truth.**
Proverbs 3:5-6.

Think back on this last week. Ask God to show you a time when you reacted outside of the fruit of the Spirit. Then walk through the steps to truth under the Galatians 5:22-23 Gauge at left, and do a Word Search. Write your experience here or in your journal.

_____
_____
_____
_____
_____
_____

Jesus said, "I am … the Truth." John 14:6a

 22

Get in the habit

of using the Galatians 5:22-23 Gauge to expose enemy lies so the truth will set you free, and Word searches to seal freedom in your heart.

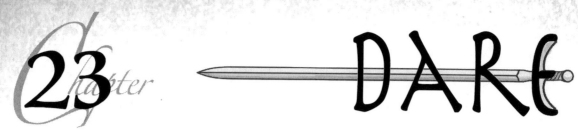

Chapter 23

DARE

to shut the door on the enemy

The battle is real

Each time God sets me free from a stronghold, the experience is different. Some journeys are longer than others. In fact, pride took almost a year to come down, and I'm still finding pieces of it I hadn't discovered before.

But the difference is *that stronghold no longer controls how I think and react.* When the pride thoughts come, I can recognize them now and choose to walk in the Spirit instead. But before, I reacted before I could think.

So watch for how the enemy tries to trigger your old lie again, and *stand in the truth. The stronger you stand the harder he'll fall.* Ephesians 6:13. After awhile those old thoughts won't come anymore. *Freedom will be your new norm* and Satan will give up that fight.

In Step 5 of the Gauge, we mentioned looking for any **unholy vows, a form of self-protection denying God's sovereignty over your life and setting yourself in His place as your protector.** 2 Samuel 22:3.

If a girl breaks your heart and you vow, "I'll never get married!" how might the enemy use that against you? _____

_____

Can you see how important it would be to break that vow and hand control back over to God? You can do that by **repenting** and then **renouncing your vow.** For instance, "In the name of Jesus, I break the vow 'I'll never get married,' and I release my future into God's hands, for I am His."

In the Word, vows, curses and blessings were serious business. You can do a Word Search on that if you'd like to know more. But our words carry power, whether we think they do or not. We need to *get in the habit of speaking blessings over ourselves and others.*

Some sins are **generational,** meaning **the children walk in the same issues as their parents,** forefathers, or other family members. 1 Kings 15:3, 26; 1 Kings 22:52, Exodus 20:5, 34:6-7, Numbers 14:18, Deuteronomy 5:9, Luke 11:50-51.

Is there anything like that in your own life? If so, **begin breaking that cycle now:**

1. **Forgive** those who sinned, who opened that door. Matthew 7:1-5, Proverbs 10:12.
2. **Repent** of any part you had in that sin.
3. **Renounce** the sins of your forefathers. Nehemiah 1:6, Psalm 79:8, Isaiah 61:4.
4. **Cut off any curses**. ("In the name of Jesus I renounce ..., and I cut off any curses related to or resulting from that sin.")
5. **Deal with any demons.** Mark 9:25. "In the name of Jesus, I send the spirit of (lust, insanity, anger, etc.), and any other demons involved, to the feet of Jesus to be dealt with by Him, and I forbid the enemy to ever pick on me, my family, my children or my children's children again...."
6. **Pray blessings** over your family and generations to come; and for Jesus to be your Shield and Protector. Ezekial 18, Genesis 17:7-9, Exodus 20:6, Deuteronomy 5:10, 7:9, Psalm 22:30, 24:6, 79:13, Luke 1:50.
7. **Walk in freedom**. Galatians 5:1, 25.

A generational sin common to the Israelites but also to us today is **occult** activity.

If your family experiences mental illness, suicidal thoughts, freak accidents, or overwhelming urges to flee when God is speaking, a door may have been opened to demonic activity and a spirit of death through the occult.

Even if you're unaware of any such issues, pray through this list and the above steps to close any doors to the enemy.

Satan worship, curses, apparitions, black magic/arts, black mass, white magic, neutral magic, séances, clairvoyance, mediums, divining, psychic powers, spiritism, ghosts, necromancy, conjuring spirits, fortune-telling, trance diagnosis, palm reading, tea-leaf reading, crystal balls, casting spells, astrology, Moon-many, horoscopes, zodiac signs, icons, numerology, parapsychology, enchantments, clairaudience, unholy dreams, unholy visions, fetishes, runes, amulets, talismans, mascots, unholy medals, ankhs, spells, incantations, potions, acupuncture, mysticism, Aryanism, Humanism, psychokinesis, telepathy, psychometry, mind control, second sight, mental science, self-realization, visualization, trances, yoga, mesmerism, auras, reincarnation, psychoanalysis, wizards, soothsaying, prostitution, prognosticators, psychography, transference, New Age, powwow, yin-yang, superstition, spiritualism, occult literature, the force, holistic medicine, levitation, graven images, idolatry, planchette, self-mutilation, Karma, Buddhism, Islam, Black Muslim, Hinduism, Taosim, Unity, Mormonism, omens, occult jewelry, shrines, temples, lodges, blood pacts, oaths, false cults, rock music, martial arts, evil dance, voodoo, E.S.P., mind reading, poltergeists, thought control, tattooing, cutting the body, graphology, neo-rationalism, agnosticism, atheism, iridology, reflexology, color therapy, death magic, firewalking, fanaticism, Rosicrucianism, screening, witchcraft, mind science, sorcery, precognition, autosuggestion, biofeedback, psychic healing, inner voices, Children of God, magic healing, Bahaism, Eastern Star, Hare Krishna, hypnotherapy, Roy Masters, Father Divine, soul travel, horoscope charts, eckankar, offerings to spirits, table tipping, good luck charms, incense burning

automatic writing, Magic Eight Ball, Christian Science, imaginary friend, channeling spirits, wart or bum charming, concept therapy, animism, spirit worship, Jehovah's Witnesses, Science of the Mind, Freemasonry (Masons), Swedenborgianism, Silva Mind Control, occult movies/TV shows, spiritual prostitution, Theosophical Society, Eastern religions, Order of the Arrow, death wishes/death oaths, psychic involvement, psychocybernetics, letters of protection, mental suggestion, Umbanda, Macumba, psychic phenomena, metaphysical healing, hypnosis, self-hypnosis, transcendental meditation, E.S.T. (The Forum), transactional analysis, self-help techniques, esoteric philosophy, rebellion against God, observing of the times, astral projection, Masters of Wisdom, handwriting analysis, out-of-body experience, human or animal sacrifice, materialization or apports, Unification Church, The Way International, communicating with the dead, pact with Satan or a spirit, tarot cards or other card laying, contact with familiar spirits, rod or pendulum diagnosis, humanistic psychology, holographic images, consulting spirit guides or mediums, automatic drawing or composing, massage by someone who channels spirits

dedication to a spirit, to Satan or to a cult
consciousness-expanding through drugs
Science of Creative Intelligence
charts with occult significance
vows (See James 5:12; Matt. 5:34-37.)
mental manipulation, mind-swapping

ancestor worship or veneration
fortune-telling or anything that predicts your future and has advised your life
blood subscriptions (subscribing yourself or your children to the devil)
false or demonic tongues (test by 1 John 4:1-3 and 1 Corinthians 12:3)
remote influence of the subconscious mind of others
incubi and succubae (sexual molestation by an evil spirit)

association with or possession of occult or pagan objects, relics, idols, images, artifacts or anything dedicated to spirits

religion or philosophy that denies the deity or blood atonement of Jesus (liberal theology that teaches salvation without repentance, Modem Theology, rationalistic or intellectual theology that denies the resurrection, the second coming, miracles, answers to prayer, spiritual gifts, the devil, demons, or God)

occult games (Dungeons and Dragons, Clairvoyant, Kabala, Mystic Eye, ESP, Ouija Board, Telepathy, Voodoo, Horoscope, Masters of the Universe, etc.)

initiation rites (into lodges, brotherhoods, shrines, clubs, sororities or fraternities that require taking an oath to uphold a man-made doctrine)

radiesthesia (water witching, dowsing forked sticks or other objects to locate water, oil, minerals, underground sewer and water lines, etc.)

fantasies, obsessions, other associations with vampires, draculas, werewolves or other occultic super-human manifestations

Other: _____
_____

23

Get in the Habit

of asking God if any door has been left open to Satan, and then closing it.

DARE
to walk in freedom

No longer bound

During war times, soldiers often made a circle facing out in order to set up a **perimeter,** or enemy-free zone, around a fallen man until they could get him to safety and healing.

Similarly, the ammunition in these chapters is useful for clearing out enemy interference, giving Christ His place as our Shield (rather than our own self-defensive measures), and allowing room for the Spirit of Truth to heal us and set us free. John 14:15-21.

For most lies or strongholds God sets you free from, you will notice an immediate sense of lightness, like a burden has been lifted.

Then the next time you walk into a similar situation, you will hopefully be on alert (1 Peter 1:13) and more easily respond in love through the Spirit.

For me it feels like the thoughts are now coming from the outside rather than within, so all I have to do is flick them away with my Sword. Ephesians 6:17. Whereas before it seemed I had no control over my reactions.

Eventually, those wrong thought patterns or temptations just never come again.

But that doesn't even begin to explain what freedom feels like.

How do you describe fresh air or a sunrise to a man who's been trapped in a dungeon his whole life? You have to *experience* it.

But sometimes, like that prisoner, *we think this jail is all there is.* Then when someone gives us dynamite to blow the walls down, we say, "I don't need that," or "That's dangerous!"

Pushback can be intense, as well. How did the Israelites experience yet worse persecution from their slave masters when God set their course for freedom? Exodus 4:29-6:9.

_____

How did they respond to that pushback? (6:9) _____

If God has shown you a stronghold and you've asked Him to set you free, then the enemy may try to put up a fight. It's kind of like cutting off the head of a huge python—the tail keeps on thrashing even though *the beast is defeated.* Revelation 12:10-12.

So, don't give up. *Stand firm.* Ephesians 6:10-14, Galatians 5:1. **Jesus is showing you the way out.** 1 Corinthians 10:13. *Take it!*

Read John 8:42-47, 14:6 and 14:15-17, and then interpret the cartoon on the next page.

_____

Are there any lies you continue to "chew on"? Ask God and write what comes to mind.

_____

Now walk through steps 5-7 of the Galatians 5:22-23 Gauge in Chapter 22 with Him.

This life is a journey. As you hit bumps along the way, some of the junk you hadn't noticed before in your heart may jostle to the surface. When that happens, get alone with God and get rid of it .

Write Galatians 5:1 in your own words:

_____

"Jesus answered, 'I am the _____ and the _____ and the _____.'" John 14:6a

⤙ 24 ⤚

Get in the habit of living in freedom:

†   Look for "the way out" in each temptation. 1 Corinthians 10:13.

†   Notice what the enemy is doing and do the opposite.

†   Ask God what He's doing and join Him.

†   Don't skip a quiet time.

†   Use the Galatians 5:22-23 Gauge (Chapter 22) regularly.

†   Do Word Searches (Chapter 22) on the subjects God is teaching you.

†   Keep a journal so you can return to the Truth when you need it.

†   Write the truth God shows you, especially scripture verses, on cards and put them in places you look each day, like your refrigerator, the mirror over the sink, the light switch in your room, or the dashboard of your car. **Let the truth you know sink deep into your heart and become the truth you live.**

†   Ask God to help you. The more you resist the lies, the less often they return, until you find you just don't think that way anymore.

to be filled with the Spirit

What are you full of?

While prayer walking in a closed country, my friend felt compelled by the Spirit to go down a certain street, where he happened upon a funeral. He walked through the open door, laid his hands on the corpse, prayed, and the dead man sat up, ALIVE!

A man filled with the Spirit is a powerful man, not in his own strength, but in God's.

The Spirit gives the power to heal, topple strongholds, lead people to faith, break down walls of prejudice, change a situation from bad to good, and *even change the world.*

Have you ever met Christians who overflow with the Spirit? When they speak, you feel Him speaking. When they worship, you feel Him moving. As they walk through life, lives are changed all around them. How did they get that way?

If you live surrendered to God, then His Spirit will flow through you. And if you expect Him to show up, He just might leave you awestruck.

So many people block out the movement of the Spirit because they're afraid of being too emotional or out-of-control, imagining things that aren't real or giving control to Satan. Have you ever thought that? Explain.

_____

_____

God is gentleman enough that if you don't want Him to do something miraculous or speak to you or through you, *He just might not.* Matthew 9:23-25.

Usually the places God shows up in power are where believers are expecting Him to.

Some Christians believe that if you speak in tongues, then you're filled with the Spirit; and if you can't, then you aren't. But I've met Christians who boast speaking in tongues who are bitter and hateful toward others; and others without that gift who are loving and humble, drawing people to God.

The proof of being filled with the Spirit is not in the gift, but in the fruit. Galatians 5:22-23.

Think about it. When you apply pressure to a spray can, what comes out? *Whatever's in the can.* So if anger, pride, bitterness, self-pity or something else is what you're full of, that's what comes out under pressure.

What about you? What came out of you last time you were under stress?

_____

_____

Do you want to be so full of the Spirit that when pressure hits, out comes love, joy, peace, patience and whatever Jesus is doing? _____

Invite Him into your space every moment.

I like to begin each day, even before I get out of bed, by asking God what He wants to do and willingly rearranging my schedule accordingly. I make sure to plan plenty of time for my quiet time, and then continue in conversation with Him all throughout the day, letting Him lead me wherever He's going and use me any way He desires.

Walking with Christ like that didn't happen overnight, though. I had to build those habits into my lifestyle. I had to *choose* to walk in the Spirit and *invite* Him to fill me and guide me.

One morning, as I awoke in the dark country where we work, I asked the Lord as always, "What do You want to do today?"

His answer came more specific than usual.

At 8:30 a.m. I was to call Isaiah, take a bus to his town to meet him at 11 a.m., and then take him to a certain village.

Reason rose up in me and I argued, "But Isaiah doesn't even know me; he just knows my husband. Besides, I'm a woman, so we'll need someone else to accompany us. And anyway, no one in that village will be there. They're all at a festival in another town."

But I surrendered to God all the same. At 8:30, I called Isaiah, half hoping he wouldn't answer. But he did, and by 11, I was telling him face-to-face about the family in that village where two had come to Christ.

"You want me to go there with you, don't you?" he asked. Then he stood up, grabbed his backpack, and reached for his hidden stash of tracts, asking, "What do we take with us?"

Reason spoke out again: "Well, they can't read and write, so maybe we should just take some fruit." Besides, carrying religious materials was dangerous in that country; we could be arrested, or worse.

Then the Holy Spirit convicted me, and I blurted out, "No! PRAY! And then *take whatever GOD tells you to take.*"

He grabbed some booklets and stuffed them into his backpack.

As we stood on the street waiting for our ride to the village, two girls who looked like prostitutes approached and asked to go with us. Isaiah explained that the night before, as his friend tried to get one of the girls to sleep with him, Isaiah said to her, "You don't want to do that," and then led her to Christ.

So the girl and her friend joined us, and when we arrived at the village, a daughter I'd never met because she attended school in another village was there with six of her classmates, preparing for the festival. I asked them, "Before you go, can we tell you a story?"

They listened as we storied from creation all the way through Christ. All seven girls came to the Lord that day, plus the friend of the new believer that came with us. And every one of them could read. When Isaiah opened his backpack, he had exactly enough booklets for each of them on growing as new believers.

At every turn throughout the day, I had the choice to be led by the Spirit or by my flesh and reason. *The consequences were eternal.*

Why is it important to let the Spirit take the lead? Colossians 1:28-29, 1 Corinthians 2:4-5.

_____

_____

God commands us in Ephesians 5:18b to be

_____.

Again, remember that anything the Spirit leads you to do must line up with the Word and God's character and draw people to Him (our Three-Fold Sieve from Chapter 13).

Spend time in worship today, laying all your responsibilities at Jesus' feet. Ask Him what He wants you to do, and then step out in obedience. Whatever situations or decisions you face, ask Him to guide you, fill you and speak through you. Write your experience.

_____

_____

_____

_____

_____

_____

_____

 25

Get in the Habit ...

... of surrendering to God every day, all the time and on every matter. Proverbs 3:5-6. Let Him fill you with His Spirit, so when the enemy "presses your buttons," all that comes out is Jesus.

to fight for purity

Sin's slippery slope

What does James 1:13-15 say about the slippery slope of sin? _____ leads to _____ which leads to _____.

Every Christian faces temptation. 1 Corinthians 10:12-13. Don't fall into the trap of believing it's too hard to resist. *Resisting the enemy is the very thing that makes him flee.* James 4:7, 1 Peter 5:8-9. You must get in the habit of recognizing Satan's lies, seeing his fingerprints on the temptations he tailor-makes for you, and **walking the opposite way.**

Jesus said if your mind even dwells on an inappropriate thought about a woman, you've already committed the act. Matthew 5:27-28.

And Galatians 5:19-21 warns that **impurity and sexual immorality will steal your spiritual inheritance from you**. That's a high price to pay for a moment of fleshly gratification.

So, what are some ways the enemy might trick you into slipping down? Take a moment to prayerfully answer these questions:

1. What movies have you seen or conversations have you participated in that portray women as objects to be used for sex? _____

2. What pornography or sexy ads have you lingered on? _____

3. Which sex scenes have you watched in movies or on TV rather than averting your eyes? _____

4. Which girls have you allowed to flirt with you who make you think inappropriate or lustful thoughts? _____

5. Have you ever had sex or thought excessively about it? _____

6. Have you ever been sexually abused? _____

7. Have you experienced sexual dreams that stick in your memory? _____

8. Have you been molested by a sexual spirit, especially while sleeping (succubus, incubus)? _____

9. Have you ever sought a prostitute or hooked up with someone for the purpose of sexual gratification? _____

10. Have you ever touched or fondled a woman's breasts or other private parts outside of marriage? _____

11. Have you ever sexually harassed a woman? Or pressured someone into engaging in sexual acts with you, when she said no? _____

12. Have you ever texted or talked dirty or exchanged inappropriate photos or videos? _____

13. Have you been to a strip bar or other event or party where sex was the main theme? _____

14. Have you engaged in any kind of virtual sexual encounters or played video games that aroused you sexually? _____

_____

15. Do you purposefully masturbate? What are you thinking on when you do? _____

_____

16. Are you engaged in inappropriate conversations or relationships with women online? Are you on websites to hook up with women for the purpose of sexual gratification? _____

_____

17. Are you attracted to men? Have you engaged in sexual acts with a man or entertained inappropriate thoughts about him?

_____

18. Other _____

The way the slippery slope of sin works is that once you give in, even just once, the enemy tempts you all the more. He wants to take you captive to obey him rather than the Holy Spirit. John 8:42-47, Romans 7:21-25, 2 Corinthians 10:3-5. And unfortunately, some of these encounters may have happened when you were too young to protect yourself. Satan doesn't play fair!

If you're going to stand strong against enemy assaults on your purity, you must be on the alert and fight. 1 Peter 5:8, Ephesians 6:10-13.

Have any of these excuses ever crossed your mind? *"It won't hurt to look just this once," "I can't help it. I'm a man. I need it," "She wants it," "Everyone's doing it," "I'm not lusting, I'm just appreciating the beauty God made," "I'm not hurting anyone." "Who's to know?"*

If the enemy can convince you the thoughts you dwell on and the desires you act on are not sin, then you won't take that first step to freedom: *repentance*. You need to see your sin for the cancer it is and get rid of it before it destroys you.

Prayerfully read 1 Thessalonians 4:3-8. What is God's will for you?

1. (v. 3) _____

_____

2. (v. 3) _____

_____

3. (v. 4-5) _____

_____

_____

_____

_____

4. (v. 6) _____

_____

_____

_____

5. (v. 7) _____

_____

Why is it dangerous to reject these instructions? (v. 8) Whom are you rejecting? _____

Meditate on Psalm 73:25, and then write a prayer from your heart to the Lord's.

_____

_____

_____

_____

_____

_____

_____

_____

 26

Get in the habit

of recognizing enemy assaults against your purity and what lies he's using to trick you into giving in. Ask God for His truth to topple the lies. Then repent, and do the opposite. Don't let sexual addictions destroy the abundant life Christ has for you. John 10:10, Exodus 20:3.

to turn the battle around

Offensive strategies

One day as I worshipped with others, the Lord pointed out to me a young man who secretly struggled with pornography.

I knew who he was but had never had a conversation with him, so I asked God to arrange a meeting. Within the hour, I was standing in a buffet line and he came and stood behind me.

As we talked, he told me his father had introduced him to pornography at a young age and lust had been a constant struggle, one he was about to take into his upcoming marriage.

That night, he, my husband, another Godly man and I gathered to pray for him and witness God setting him free!

If you have given in to sexual sin, and even if you are addicted, remember there is no pit too deep for God's long arm to pull you out. Do you want to be free? Tell Him.

_____
_____
_____

Everyone's journey is different, so you'll need to seek God for His path for you (Proverbs 3:5-6). But try walking through these **basic steps to turn the battle around**:

1. Agree with God that it is sin. Just because you're not married yet doesn't give you license to sin against your wife or to desecrate the temple of the Holy Spirit. Don't make excuses. Don't listen to what others say. Know the Word. See sin the way God does. Hate it. And *repent*. Here's some ammunition: 1 Thessalonians 4:3-8, Colossians 3:5-9, Ephesians 5:1-17, Galatians 5:16-25, 1 Corinthians 6:9-20, 3:16-17, Romans 6:12-19, Hebrews 13:4-

5, Matthew 5:27-28, James 4:7-8, 1:21-25, 2 Timothy 3:1-7, 2:20-22.

2. Ask the Lord when and how that sin first entered your life. *Most sexual strongholds have their origin in isolation, emptiness, father wounds, or feelings of not measuring up.* So don't be surprised if the memory He brings to mind is such a wound. Remember what you felt when that happened and look for the lies (John 8:42-47, 2 Corinthians 10:3-5), then ask God for His truth. *This is the truth that will set you free.* So, stay in that moment with the Lord until He answers you. (See the Gauge and Search in Chapter 22.)

3. Whatever void you were trying to fill, ask God to fill it with Himself and with the the holy opposite (acceptance, love, joy, peace, purpose, self-control, the Spirit....).

4. Ask the Lord to show you any open doors in your family line with regard to sexual sin, and follow the steps in Chapter 23.

5. Tell any demons of lust, pornography, infidelity, etc., they must flee in the name of Jesus. Then pray for God's covering over your marriage and future generations.

6. Forgive anyone who may have introduced that sin into your life, pray for him/her and bless him/her.

7. Ask the Lord to bring to mind those you have had inappropriate thoughts about (Matthew 5:27-28) or have engaged in sexual acts with. Because of 1 Corinthians 6:12-20, cut off any physical, spiritual, mental, emotional, sexual, etc., ties to that person and any strongholds that entered your life because of that union. For instance, *"Forgive me, Lord, for my sin and for leading _____ into sin. In*

the name of Jesus, I cut off any unholy ties to _____, and release her (him) to receive Your forgiveness and mercy and to have a blessed marriage founded on You..." Spend time praying for her and for your own marriage.

8. Pray cleansing prayers through your home, especially your bedroom, bathroom, living room or other places where you are often tempted, asking God to send out anything unclean and to fill your home with His presence. Deuteronomy 7. Declare each room as holy unto the Lord and cancel any rights the enemy might feel he has to bother you because of acts done by you or former tenants. Pray special blessings over your bed, asking God to protect your dreams and fill them with Himself. Play worship music throughout your home day and night, and sing along.

9. Sexual strongholds go both ways. If you have done the above and God has given you a measure of freedom, but you experience an overwhelming draw to turn your head and think lustful thoughts about a woman (advertisement, man, etc.) she might have a sexual stronghold and the demons assigned to draw men to the thought of her could be tugging at you. Ephesians 6:12. Try saying under your breath, "If this is the enemy, stop it in the name of Jesus!" Then pray for that woman's freedom, salvation and however God leads. **If you pray more for eternal matters when the enemy attacks than when he leaves you alone,** *he'll eventually leave you alone!*

10. Don't let shame and self-condemnation overwhelm you. If you fall, receive God's forgiveness, forgive yourself, let God show you what thoughts led you to fall so you can learn, and then get up and walk again!

~~ 27 ~~

Get in the Habit

of fixing your eyes on Christ whenever you feel empty, lonely, unaccepted, incompetent, bored or whatever else drives you to give in to impure thoughts. Close your eyes, block out everything around you, picture the Lord seated on His throne (Revelation 1:12-18) and worship Him.

to guard your heart, mind and body

New mind, new habits

Walking through the steps in the last chapter will open the way for freedom no matter the origin of your struggles.

But **to live free, you must retrain your thought patterns.** Galatians 5:1. As you read through this chapter, highlight or underline ways God is calling you to renew your mind. Romans 12:1-2.

In 1 Timothy 5:1-2, how are you to treat older women? _____.
Younger women? _____.
Both men and women? _____.

Take a moment to think through all your relationships. Is there anyone you are not treating as a sister or brother with "all purity"?

_____

_____

_____

You were created for oneness, intimacy, love, acceptance, worth, belonging, power....

But **those holes are God-sized**. If you try to fill them with lust, pornography, masturbation, homosexuality or other sexual acts, you will come up empty. Like a drug, sexual addictions take over your thoughts, decisions and whole life to bow to their cravings. Then shame, guilt, defeat, emptiness and broken relationships destroy your abundant life in Christ. John 10:10. *Don't give in!*

Take a moment to ask the Lord what heart issues trigger sexual temptation for you. Isolation? Low self-esteem? Father wounds? Failure? A sense of powerlessness? Write what He brings to mind. _____

_____

The most powerful deterrent to temptation is

a deep, vibrant relationship with God.

"When I only listen to non-Christian music or when I'm distracted by YouTube and gaming, I start to stumble," says one young man of God. "But spending my free time doing things that pertain to God helps me focus on Him, distracting me from the ways of the world until all I want is God.

"To get back on track, I force myself to have devotions even when I don't want to; I pray for God to help me yearn for that time with Him all the more; and I surround myself with friends who lead my conversations to God.

"We need to go to God as we are. He has grace for what we've done and He alone can help us out of that pit. Thinking that if you clean up your act you'll have a better spiritual life doesn't work. But if you have a spiritual life, then the rest of your life will clean up, and then your spiritual life will get better."

Are any of those suggestions helpful to you? What other ways have you found to keep your mind, heart and body on track?

_____

_____

_____

Read Proverbs 28:13 and James 5:16. What is God saying to you about secret sin?

_____

_____

_____

_____

Lust grows in isolation, secrecy and darkness. That **isolation must be eliminated in order for you to live in freedom.**

This is not to say you shouldn't have time alone. Everyone needs time alone, especially with God. But it is what you do with that time that matters.

Fix your eyes on the Lord, worship Him only. If your mind begins to wander, don't just think you can will yourself to stop. *Your willpower isn't enough to break free from lust.* **You need Someone stronger.** So **hand your thoughts over to the Lord**. 2 Corinthians 10:3-5. Go back through Steps 2-3 in the last chapter. It's likely there are more lies God wants to set you free from.

Get an accountability partner who will ask you the hard questions, pray for you and with you regularly and help you draw closer to the Lord. Put his number on speed dial for those times when you're struggling.

If pornography tempts you, **install an alert program** on your computer to send a report of the websites you've visited to your accountability partner. If you've seen pornography, repent and **cut off any ties to those images**. Ask God to cleanse your mind and give you a new start. Follow His directions for the specific path to freedom He's asking you to walk, like only using your computer in public places.

If your thoughts toward women are not brotherly but lustful, take time to ask the Lord why. What lies do you believe about women? When did those thoughts first come in? **Ask God for His truth.** (Steps 2-3 in Chapter 27).

Choose to **close or avert your eyes** from inappropriate advertisements or movie scenes.

Learn to **recognize when you're weak and**

receive God's grace. 2 Corinthians 12:9-10.

Whenever sexual thoughts come across your mind, if you didn't invite them, don't let them worry you. It's lingering or warring with your will that makes the battle worse. Hand your thoughts to God and then worship Him, read the Word, pray for others, or call a friend. Place your *focus on the One you love.*

If your friends are going out, don't just go along. **Ask where they're going and what they'll do there.** Then **ask God** what to do.

If a girl who spells danger is headed for you, **go the other way**. If she calls, tell her you're busy and **hang up**. If she texts or messages, **block it**. If the draw to her is overwhelming, try Step 9 from the last chapter.

Work hard to **stay away from alone situations with a girl**, especially at night. Hang out instead together in groups with other friends.

You are not yours to give away, and neither is that daughter of the King you're attracted to, until the day He gives His consent and you are married. 1 Corinthians 6:12-20. So,

Look at every woman as a sister of Christ. Treat her with dignity, respect and absolute purity, as Jesus would.

The wife God gives you will be a precious treasure. **Guard your kisses and your body** as a wedding gift to her and her alone as long as you both live. Remember, *she is looking for a Godly man* too.

28

Get in the habit

of having others with you whenever you are with a woman. If you find yourself alone with her, keep the door open, call a friend and ask him to come, invite her to go with you someplace public. Seek friendship with women, rather than an exclusive relationship that blocks out your friends, God and any thought but her. Touch is a trigger that will drive you to want more, so guard against starting something that is soon to escalate. Remember God is watching you. This is His precious daughter He loves and honors and wants to save in all purity for her husband. And He also wants to keep you pure for your wife. Ask Him to help you overcome your weakness and to show you the "way of escape" every time you are tempted. 1 Corinthians 10:13.

DARE
to have faith

Moving those mountains

"He who believes in Me, the works that I do he will do also; and greater works than these he will do, because I go to My Father. And whatever you ask in My name, that I will do."
John 14:12-13

I remember one Fourth of July, as we drove from one city to another, our seven-year-old asked God for fireworks. Within minutes, the sky lit up with *flashes of lightning all around us* in the most spectacular display of His glory.

But God didn't stop there. As we started over a bridge, the traffic jammed and we had to stop *because of the fireworks.* He had given us the best view in the city!

I know now why Jesus said we must be like little children. Mark 10:13-16. **Children have no problem believing that their Heavenly Daddy can do anything.**

But often, the older we get the colder our faith. Because we let Satan use life experiences to cloud our view of a loving, omnipotent God and sow seeds of doubt in our hearts.

In fact, each of the temptations Satan fired at Jesus in Matthew 4:1-11 began with *"If ..."*

But Jesus answered, *"It is written ...."*

Follow your Master's lead. Don't give in to doubt. James 1:2-8. Know what God's Word says, stand on it and use it as an offensive weapon against the enemy. Ephesians 6:17-18.

God is and always has been sovereign, wise, good, slow to anger, just, merciful, all-powerful, and everything else Scripture says He is. And you are beloved and accepted by Him.

You might doubt your own ability, but never, ever doubt God's power or love. 1 Corinthians 2:4-5. Colossians 1:28-29. Philippians 4:13. 2 Corinthians 12:9-10.

Your faith must be in God, not in circumstances, others, yourself, or even in what you want God to do.

One woman I mentored struggled with trusting her husband. When we did a Word Search on "trust," we found hundreds of Scriptures that say, *"Trust in the Lord,"* but only a handful that say, *"Don't trust in man," "Don't trust in armies (riches, etc.)."*

In other words, **trusting anything or anyone but God isn't really supposed to be our thought.** Not that you shouldn't trust your spouse or friend. Just, *trust God.* Period.

Rest in the assurance that God is in control, that He is good and that He will bring the best out of every circumstance. Romans 8:28.

How does faith in God make the impossible possible? See Matthew 21:21-22.

_____

_____

God is so God. Believe that He can and will perform a miracle, but don't be surprised if the miracle isn't what you expect it to be.

You may have faith for Him to heal someone physically, but He may be all about healing him spiritually; or the miracle might be what He does in your own heart as you pray.

Jesus asked God to take the cup of suffering from Him, but His faith was in God, not in God releasing Him from death on the cross. He qualified His request with surrender to God's will. Mark 14:38.

If God calls you to be a missionary in a war-torn country, will He protect you and your family? Most certainly! The protection may be physical or it may be spiritual. You may indeed face torture or death for His name's sake. But remember this:

The safest place to be is in God's hands.

Don't fear what people may do to you. Luke 12:4-7. This life is short anyway, and full of difficulties and trials no matter what country you live in. **Trust in God, follow Him wherever He leads you, love Him with all your heart, and live as if heaven is your home.**

A man of faith is a man at rest because his eyes are on the Lord. Isaiah 30:15, Joshua 1:9, 2 Chronicles 20:12. He knows in Whom he trusts, and that makes him a man of courage.

Did you notice Jesus slept in the raging storm first, and *then* He calmed it? Matthew 8:23-27. *Trust in the Lord who holds all things in His hand, and your heart will be at rest no matter what rages about you.*

Years ago, most sick people I prayed for actually got worse. I developed a complex, in fact, about my apparent lack of the gift of healing. Whenever believers gathered to pray for the sick, I stood silently in the back.

Of course, the lie in there is obvious. **Whether or not a person is healed is not dependent on my wonderful or terrible prayer skills or my gifting or my faith (see that word "my"), but on the ONE WHO HEALS.**

We were prayer walking a Buddhist temple one night, when one of the men with us cried out in pain and couldn't move. He had injured his knee two weeks earlier and well-known intercessors had prayed for him to no avail. Now the pain had become unbearable.

Surrounded by monks chanting to demons and throngs of people bowing to idols, I laid my hand on his and spoke out the words I felt God saying. And *God healed him!*

But He did more than that. **He declared in** the midst of His enemies that HE ALONE IS GOD. And He showed me **how He can move the mountains in my heart.**

The key to asking for something in Jesus' name is to walk so closely with Him that you know His heart and what He is doing. John 14:10-21. *Then when He wants to perform a miracle, you won't miss the show.*

Ask God if there is any way doubt and fear are strangling your faith. Look for the lies, and ask Him for His truth, saying "Help my unbelief." Mark 9:14-32. Write your prayer and what He shows you here.

_____

_____

_____

_____

What difficult decisions or circumstances are you or someone you know facing?

_____

_____

_____

Ask God what He wants to do, pray as He leads, surrender to His will and trust Him for the outcome. Believe Him to do something miraculous, even if it's not the miracle you're looking for. Write your prayer here.

_____

_____

_____

_____

_____

_____

_____

 29

Get in the habit

of walking so close to Jesus that you know what His heart is, so that when you pray it is through His Spirit for the things He has already planned to do. Ask Him for the big things as well as the small, and expect an answer that just might blow you away. John 15:7.

to shrink not from death

Dying to live

Has it ever baffled you how the Word tells us to count it "pure joy" when we suffer? James 1:2, 1 Thessalonians 1:6, 1 Peter 4:13. What's so fun about suffering?

Paul was stoned for preaching and his body was dragged outside the city. But the believers gathered around him and prayed; and then *he got up and went on preaching*. What did he say to the disciples? Acts 14:21-22. Why is that "encouraging"?

_____

_____

_____

_____

_____

2 Timothy 3:12 says that everyone who wants to live a Godly life will be persecuted. It's not a "maybe" or a "hopefully not," but *a promise you can count on.*

John 15:20 reminds us we are no greater than our Master. If Jesus endured persecution for His love for God and obedience to Him, then we His servants can expect it also.

Our hope, our joy, in Christ is that every trial, persecution and difficulty we face in this life will gain us eternal rewards if we keep our eyes fixed on Him and go through the trial His way. 2 Corinthians 4:17-18; James 1:2-4.

Before we moved overseas, whenever I heard reports of persecution of believers in the place where God was calling us, I remember crying out to Him, "How do they do it? I don't know that I could go through torture, solitary confinement or seeing my family beaten before my eyes."

He answered, "You know you would much rather be in a jail cell with Me than anywhere else without Me."

And He's right. I know that the safest place to be is in His hands. He is my Everything. Without His presence, life holds no meaning.

"For to me, to live is Christ, and to die is gain."
Philippians 1:21

Persecution may mean physical death, as it does for many believers throughout the world. Or it may mean death to your reputation, a relationship, your job, your dreams or something else of deep value.

But I want to challenge you to a radical kind of death — **the Galatians 2:20 LIFE:**

"I have been crucified with Christ; it is no longer I who live, but Christ lives in me; and the life which I now live in the flesh I live by faith in the Son of God, who loved me and gave Himself for me."

In each trial you face, God may ask you to "die" to something that is not of Him, and be "resurrected" into the opposite, which is freedom and life in Him.

For example, when others attack you, you may find the Lord urging you to die to your need for man's approval and come alive knowing you are fully accepted, loved and even delighted in by the King of Kings.

Read Philippians 3:7-10. What is considered loss in comparison to the greatness of knowing Jesus and following Him?

_____

Jesus thought nothing of His stature as God when He crammed Himself into a mortal human body. He *chose* to die. What did He gain? See Philippians 2:1-18; Hebrews 2:5-18.

_____

I hope you read those last two passages, because they're powerful!

What does Jesus call us in John 15:9-17? How did He show He meant what He said?

In light of that, what should your response be to the One who loves you like that?

In Colossians 3:1-14, what do we die to?

And what do we come alive to?

In James 1:12, the "crown of _____" rewards those who endure persecution.

*"Do not be afraid of what you are about to suffer. I tell you, the devil will put some of you in prison to test you, and **you will suffer persecution. ... Be faithful, even to the point of death, and I will give you LIFE as your victor's crown**."* Revelation 2:10

This reward belongs to those who are faithful until death, serving God well through suffering, enduring when tempted, dying to themselves and giving their lives for His sake.

In what ways have you been persecuted by people or the enemy for obeying Christ?

Are you facing persecution now? Ask God how He wants you to walk through this trial. Is there something in you that is not of Him — some desire, sin, thought process or judgment that He wants you to die to?

Ask Him to replace that death in you with the opposite that is life (truth for lies, God's approval for man's, grace for judgment, selflessness for selfishness, etc.). Write your prayer here.

*"Then I heard a loud voice saying in heaven, 'Now salvation, and strength, and the kingdom of our God, and the power of His Christ have come, for the accuser of our brethren, who accused them before our God day and night, has been cast down. And **they overcame him by the blood of the Lamb and by the word of their testimony, and they did not love their lives (so much as to shrink from) death.** Therefore rejoice, O heavens, and you who dwell in them! Woe to the inhabitants of the earth and the sea! For the devil has come down to you, having great wrath, because he knows that he has a short time.'"* Revelation 12:10-12

⟿ 30 ⟾

Get in the habit

of daily dying to those things in you that are not of God so you can come ALIVE to the life-giving things of Christ.

Part 4

"Those who live according to the flesh set their minds on the things of the flesh, but those who live according to the Spirit, the things of the Spirit. ... For if you live according to the flesh you will die; but if by the Spirit you put to death the deeds of the body, you will live. ... For we are more than conquerors through Him who loved us. ... If we live in the Spirit, let us also walk in the Spirit."

Romans 8:5-37, Galatians 5:25

Living for the King

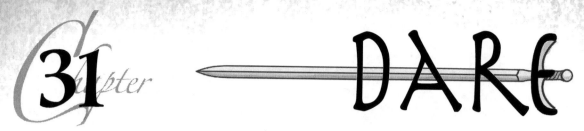

31 Chapter

to share Christ with the lost

Hey! No hoarding!

You've been given the most valuable gift of all time—salvation. You didn't do anything special to earn it. Christ did it all. Ephesians 2:8-9; Matt 13:44-46; 1 John 3:1-3. *You carry within you the Treasure of Christ.* 2 Corinthians 4:6-7. **Don't hoard your Treasure!**

What has Christ given you? Forgiveness. Heaven. Life. Freedom. Joy. Peace. Love. The list goes on. Each jewel is priceless. *People have killed to gain even just one of those things.* If you don't believe me, check out the news.

Jesus is the answer to everything people on this earth are looking for. But so many still haven't heard this Good News.

When we were first married, God called us to an international church in a university city. Most of the people who attended were unbelievers from closed countries. They came to practice English, but mostly they wanted to know Who this Jesus was that their governments had forbidden them to learn about.

A few years of that was enough to propel us out into the darkest corners of the world where no one would hear unless we went.

Was it hard to leave our home country? No, not really. Because Jesus is our Home. *Wherever He is, that's where we want to be.* And if He's leading us into a turbulent nation, then that's where we're headed with Him.

When I get to heaven, I want to see a throng of thousands before the throne because I was faithful, because I didn't hoard my Treasure, but gave it away.

Not that I shared with all those thousands. But I shared with this one, who shared with that one, who shared with ten, and poof! Thousands dancing at the feet of Jesus.

In the closed country where we live, a local girl joined me hiking one day. I pointed to the mountains and said, "Do you know Who made those?"

"No. They've just always been there."

I shared with her about the Creator God Who loves her, and she said, "If there's a God like that, then I want to love Him back. But my village must not be very important, because we've never heard this news before."

And yet, it is precisely because she and her village are beloved by God that He arranged our meeting that day in the wilderness!

What if I'd stayed home relaxing that day? Actually, I would have if that's what God was leading me to do; Jesus rested, too sometimes. But He also did *whatever His Father led Him to do every moment*. And that's the point.

What is the "Great Commission"? Write out Matthew 28:19-20.

_____

_____

_____

_____

Some Christians argue that Jesus gave this command to His disciples only; it's not for us. But I would argue that *anything written in the Word that is the heart of God is most certainly a word for us today.*

How many people have not gone to the mission field because they don't feel "called"? Perhaps our response should rather be, *"I will go, Lord, unless You call me to stay."*

Okay. That's my plug for missions. But don't feel guilty if you're one of the ones God has called to stay. Just, *wherever you are, make the most of every opportunity to share Him with others.* Ephesians 5:15-16.

He has freely forgiven you; now forgive others. He has freely loved you; now love others. And as He has freely set you free from your sin, now share with others so they too can be forgiven and go to heaven.

Don't let fear of what others think of you keep you from sharing Christ's love with them. Let love rule you, not fear. 1 John 4:18.

Remember, **they are lost and headed for hell without Jesus.** It's not about them liking you. It's about *Jesus*, who loved them so much He gave His life to save them. If you truly love them, you will tell them this Good News.

Traveling alone to speak at a conference in South America, my assigned seat landed me next to a burly soccer player from Argentina. As soon as the plane took off, his face drained of color, his hands gripped the armrests and he rattled off a stream of Hail Marys.

I silently asked the Lord for an open door to share about His perfect love. 1 John 4:18.

The man looked over at me. "Why aren't you afraid?" he asked. *Ding! Door open!*

Although Catholic and religious, he had never heard the meat of the Gospel. As I shared, his hands eased their grip off the armrests, the color returned to his face, and before the plane landed, *he prayed to receive Christ!*

Leading someone to the Lord doesn't always happen that quickly, though. I shared 25 years with my best friend from high school before she finally gave her heart to Him. In the end, it was our family's joy and love that spoke louder than words to her. But she had needed to see it all those years to experience Truth.

It's important that you follow God's lead as you share with others, because each person's situation is unique. He may want you to share certain portions of your testimony (how He's changed your life) that relate specifically to what they're going through.

But a **basic outline of the Gospel message** you can share with the lost is this:

1. God loves you and has a plan for your life. And it is good. Jeremiah 29:11-13.

2. Sin separates us from God. Romans 6:23.

3. Jesus provided the way for us to be restored to God through His death on the cross. John 3:16.

4. If we confess our sins, believe in Jesus and follow Him, God forgives us and gives us eternal life. Romans 10:9.

One great door opener to soften people's hearts to hear about Jesus is **prayer evangelism**. When others share a problem with you, ask if you can pray for them. If they say yes, then do it right there on the spot. When God answers that prayer, they'll be astounded at His love and power and want to know more about Him. In fact, when my friend prayed for a blind girl, *even though she wasn't healed,* her family was so overwhelmed by God's love through my friend they all accepted Christ!

Read Romans 10:13-15. What do you feel God saying to your heart?

Write in your journal the names of those you know who don't believe in Jesus yet. How will you share His love this week? Ask God, and write what He brings to mind. Pray for them daily and let God empower you to share.

༒ 31 ༒

Get in the habit

of looking for open doors to share the love of Christ. Then walk through them without fear, asking the God who created each person and loves them beyond measure to empower you and speak through you in just the way they will easily understand.

Chapter 32

DARE

to feed God's sheep

A banquet of love and grace

My great grandmother cooked for railroad workers in the early 1900s. She served them quite a feast: mashed potatoes and gravy, corn, roast beef, biscuits, peas, apple pie.... But she and my great grandfather also served them a *spiritual banquet*. No one left their table without hearing how much Christ loves them.

In John 21:15-17, what did Jesus say we would do if we love Him? _____
_____. And some versions of Jeremiah 50:7 (NIV) call the Lord our "true pasture.

All around you are hungry people. Jesus is the answer to their every problem — the only One who will fill their empty places. So *give them Jesus.*

Let the name "Jesus" be the most common word in your vocabulary. If you truly love others, Matthew 22:37-39, you will share with them the things God has taught you so they can know Him in deeper ways, too.

It's those spontaneous moments that awe me the most—when I find myself way too transparent with people I don't know, telling them some story of how God pulled me out of a pit. Suddenly, I see tears rolling down their cheeks and they blurt out, "That's just what I'm struggling with! How did you know?"

But I didn't know, and that's how remarkable this partnership with God is. He alone knows just which clump of His Pasture someone needs at the very moment they need it.

If you are walking with Christ and your heart is ready and willing to say and do anything He wants, He will astound you with the ways He uses you to transform lives.

So don't shy away from teaching a Bible study or preaching if it's something God's asking you to do, even if you feel you'll be no good at that. It's not about you. *It's about walking close to the One you love and sharing your Portion with others who hunger for Him.*

In fact, leadership is a great way for you to go deeper in the Lord yourself, especially if you know you can't do it without Him. *The more ill-equipped you feel to do something God calls you to do, the more likely you are to lean on Him* rather than your own ability or experience.

It is precisely such **humility** that **invites the Holy Spirit to empower you.** 2 Corinthians 12:9-10. But if you think you already know what you're doing, *you're likely to do it in your own strength and miss the miracle.*

That time you spend at the Lord's feet as you prepare and listen for His leading will be some of your most intimate times with Him, especially because *sometimes you need to learn the lesson yourself first before you teach it.*

Here are some **tips for Spirit-led feeding of God's sheep** (See more in Chapter 43):

- As you prepare, ask God what He wants to say. Listen for His answer so you can **come in line with His purposes**.

- **Pray in the days prior to the Bible study for the people who will attend**. Ask God to meet them in powerful and personal ways and to give them a hunger for Him.

- Get to the meeting place 30 minutes or more ahead to pray and **invite God to do anything He wants to do** and to fill the room with His presence. I like to touch each chair and pray for God's special touch on whoever will sit there.

- **Begin with worship** to invite God's felt

presence and help participants focus on Him. Various forms of audio-visual music with lyrics are available on-line, or just do it live.

- **Invite those who come to ask God personally to speak to their hearts.** Only He knows what they're struggling with and what they need to hear from Him.

- Continue praying and listening to God throughout the Bible study, so that **if He moves in a new direction you can follow Him there.**

- Pray afterward for God to **seal His truth in their hearts and give them courage to walk out in it.**

Take a moment now to ask God, "What opportunities do I have to feed Your sheep?" Write what comes to mind. Is there a small group that needs a leader? Are there some friends you want to study this book or another Bible study together with? Is there an opportunity to lead worship? Are there people He wants you to encourage? _____ _____ _____ _____

What has God been teaching you in your daily quiet times and how has He transformed you this week? _____ _____ _____ _____

How will you share that with others? Ask God to show you, and write His instructions. _____ _____ _____

"Jesus said ... 'Do you truly love me?... Feed my sheep.'" John 21:15-17

Get in the Habit

of sharing with others what Jesus is teaching you. Not only will it help you remember that truth and walk out in it, but most Christians are spiritually starved. They're not worshipping, reading the Word or listening to God on a regular basis. But if you're sharing some of your banquet food with them, they just might see how good He tastes, and head to His table for more.

33 Chapter DARE

~ to care about the needs of others

Empowered by love

One day, after hiking many miles through the mountains of the closed country where we live, I was tired, thirsty and hungry. An old woman rested by the road, her load of vegetables on the ground beside her.

Prompted by the Spirit (although anyone else might have thought lunacy), I offered to carry her burden, hoisted the oversized load of squash onto my shoulders and followed her up a narrow mountain path to her village.

Higher and higher we climbed. Unaccustomed to heavy labor, my back ached and I found it hard to lift my legs. Inside, I cried out to the God who had asked me to do this crazy feat, and He strengthened me.

At last, after a climb that would take me a week to recover from, we arrived at the woman's home. She faced me, tears streaming down the crevices of her face. "I'm 83 years old, and no one has ever done anything like that before for me. Why did you do it?"

For the first time in her hard life, that precious woman heard God's name and saw His love for her in action.

"Bear one another's burdens." Galatians 6:2a

Jesus said every kindness shown to others is a kindness done unto Him. Matthew 25:31-46. In fact, the good things you do are evidence you are His. Ephesians 2:10.

Helping others is an act of worship.

In the middle ages, knights lived by a code of conduct called "chivalry." During a violent time in history, they were expected to not only be skilled at combat to defend king and kingdom, but also to

- help the helpless
- defend the weak
- show courtesy to others
- be gallant toward women
- show loyalty to their king
- be humble
- serve God at all times
- offer mercy to a vanquished enemy
- live a life that brought honor to their king

That's not unlike the code your King has asked you to live by as a man of God. Based on Micah 6:8, Isaiah 1:17, and Jeremiah 22:3, write out your King's code for you.

_____

_____

_____

A man of God doesn't just look out for himself. Philippians 2:4. *He has a servant's heart that looks out for others.* Philippians 2:5-8.

If selfishness rules you, you will drown in it, never satisfied. But if you love the Lord with all your heart and love others, serving them empowered by God's love, then you will find fulfillment and joy. Romans 13:11-14; Ephesians 4:2-3, 29-32.

Seek to love more than to be loved,
to understand more than to be understood,
to give more than to receive,
to serve more than to be served.

As I was writing this chapter, a friend in need called from the hospital. Was helping her inconvenient? You bet! My husband was on a trip and I needed to fix supper for our kids. The traffic was terrible. And it stormed lightning, thunder and torrents of rain—which I had to ride in on my bike.

But God was magnificent. Not only did He minister through me (bringing her just the meal she craved, working out money details, finding her a caretaker), but the ride home was spectacular. I breathed in the sweet, fresh fragrance of the rain that slapped my face and worshipped God, praying for the lost people I passed and asking Him to soften the "soil" of their parched hearts.

If I hadn't fixed my eyes on Him, though, I might have feared being struck by lightning or losing control on the slippery streets. I might have felt perturbed at the cold rain soaking me and stinging my eyes; or inconvenienced by the timing and distance I had to travel.

I needed to look through His eyes at every turn to love through His powerful love.

"And though I bestow all my goods to feed the poor… but have not love, it profits me nothing."
1 Corinthians 13:3

When love for the God who calls you to help others empowers you and He is the one you meet as you worship Him with your life out there, then it's not a burden to carry your brother's; it is exciting and wonderful.

"Let all that you do be done in love."
1 Corinthians 16:14

What are some practical things you can do this week to care for the needs of others?

_____

_____

_____

Get in the Habit

of listening to others, caring about their feelings, and looking for ways to bless them or help them in their time of need. Ask God questions like, "Lord, how can I bless my mother today?" or "What can I do to help that family or friend?" Then let Him lead you. When you have a servant's heart, you look a lot like Jesus. Philippians 2:1-16.

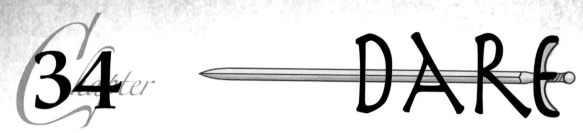

34

DARE

to mentor and be mentored

Mentored see, mentored do

What did Paul ask the believers he discipled to do? See 1 Corinthians 4:16.

_____

Is there anyone you have looked up to in the Lord? What good habits have you learned from that person?

_____

_____

_____

Whom does Ephesians 5:1 say we should imitate? _____.

That's a pretty tall order, isn't it? Matthew 5:48 says, *"Be _____, therefore, as your heavenly Father is _____."*

It's one thing to imitate a person. But *God*? He's the One Who made us. Surely He knows we're flawed and sinful. How does He expect us to be perfect like He is?

Pray as you read Hebrews 10:14, and write what you feel God saying.

_____

_____

This verse has become one of my life verses, because it totally sets me free to run with all my heart after God. My mistakes have been covered and I'm already "made" (past tense: it's already done!) perfect in God's eyes because of what Christ has done for me.

Now the adventure is "being made" (present passive: it's in the process) holy—set apart to Him, pure, dedicated to Him. **It's about relationship, not performance.**

1 Peter 1:16 is another "copy-me" verse: *"Be _____ because I am _____."*

That sounds like a tall order, too. But what amazing God-thing do we get to set our hope on that takes the stress totally out of that command and makes it a joy? See 1 Peter 1:13-16.

_____

_____

God freely gives us His favor out of His bountiful heart of love, not because we deserve it, but simply *because of what Christ has done for us.* The result for us on the receiving end is unspeakable joy and gratefulness.

So now, the Word has set us up with the ultimate Mentor. He is the One we listen to and follow and imitate and run after. And our journey is Him. He is setting us apart more and more for His purposes to become more and more like Him as we fall deeper and deeper in love with Him. 2 Corinthians 3:17-18.

It is dangerous to become stagnant in your walk with God.

Think about it. What grows in stagnant pools? Bacteria and germs that make you sick. But the stream that flows from the Source is clear, life-giving, pure. It swells with the fullness of the Living Waters that flow into it, and spreads across the land of our hearts, transforming it into a place where things grow and thirst is quenched. Ezekial 47:1-12.

One of the most valuable keys to growing and "flowing" in Christ all your life is to surround yourself with mature, Godly people who have been through the hard things and have come out victorious.

When someone close to Jesus shares with me a difficulty he's gone through, I get to know God deeper through his trial. I can soak in the truth he teaches me that God taught him, letting it become a part of who I am as I walk out in it, as well, even though I never went through the trial myself.

It's like what I overheard our son tell his little sister: *"You can learn by listening to Mom and Dad's advice, or you can learn the hard way—by messing up. Either way you learn. But the first way's much easier."*

Another good reason to have a mentor in your life is **accountability**. He can dig into the Word with you, share his own experiences, pray for you and encourage you; or question your theology if you're headed in the wrong direction. 2 Timothy 3:10-17.

He can also ask you the hard questions and help you stand strong. If you're tempted to misuse the Internet, for example, he might ask, "Have you been on the Internet this week? What did you do there?"

Paul encourages us to mentor others, too:

"The things that you have heard from me… commit these to faithful men who will be able to teach others also." 2 Timothy 2:2

As you grow closer to God, He will show you new wonders in His Word. Hebrews 4:12-13; 2 Timothy 3:16-17. What you have received from Him is not just for you, but also for the body of Christ. 2 Corinthians 1:3-4. So don't be afraid to **mentor others**. And don't worry about doing it "wrong." Different people mentor in different ways. I like to encourage believers to walk in truth, freedom and oneness with Christ. Can you tell?

My parents were my first mentors. They taught me about prayer, faith, love, truth and values I will carry with me all my life. Another woman opened me up to deeper depths of God's love. Others taught me the power of worship and walking in the Spirit. Several more helped me tear down strongholds so I could help others do the same. And some amazing mothers helped me parent wisely.

God has brought a string of incredible models into my life. But *my first model is Jesus.*

Anything someone else teaches me must match God's Word and His character, or I'm not going to imitate it.

Who are some Christians you look up to? What are some Godly things you see in their character? Ask God if any of these or someone else is a mentor He has planned for you.

_____

_____

Who are less mature believers you know? Are any of them hungry for God? Ask the Lord to make it clear to both of you if He wants you to mentor someone.

_____

Mentoring can be done one-on-one, in a group or just casually through hanging out with someone and speaking truth into his life in conversation and in the way you live. Ask God to show you how He wants you to be mentored and to mentor.

_____

_____

_____

_____

Word of caution: Don't mentor a woman one-on-one if she's not someone you plan to marry. Praying together can feel intimate, and the enemy may use those feelings to tempt you with physical intimacy.

34

Get in the Habit

of asking God how you need to look more like Him. Then look for believers around you who walk well in that aspect of His character. Ask them how they do that and what journey they went through to get there. Surround yourself with people who act like Jesus, and you will find it easier to be like Him too.

to model Proverbs 3:5-6

Not my way, His way

You are a leader, whether you want to be or not. *Every decision and choice you make, no matter how big or small, influences others.*

If your influence could lead people to do the most important thing of all, what would that be? _____

_____

What if everyone around you loved God, knew the Word and lived out what it says? James 1:22. What if Kingdom Culture love became the norm in the culture you live in? Matthew 22:37-40. How different would friendships, marriages and families be? How might society change? _____

_____

_____

That may seem like an impossible dream, and yet, if you live an empowered life through Christ, *you will make a difference in this world.*

My greatest desire is to walk as one with Christ and to influence others to do the same. Why do you think Proverbs 3:5-6 would be a key passage for that? _____

_____

_____

Take a moment here to go ahead and write out Proverbs 3:5-6 and memorize it.

_____

_____

_____

_____

_____

_____

One way to influence others to walk in the fullness of that passage is to do it yourself.

Don't lean on your own understanding as you make daily decisions and walk through life; look to God. Ask Him what He wants to do and follow Him there.

Then others will see you flowing in the Spirit and desire His empowering too.

As you go through your problems, **share with others what God is teaching you.**

And instead of asking others for advice, **let them see you go to God first.**

But the most powerful way to influence others to walk as one with Christ is to *lead them into that relationship themselves.*

It's natural when someone comes to you for advice to give it. We like to feel important or needed, so we share our experiences hoping others won't make the same mistakes.

But what if, instead of giving them your own solutions to their problem, you *lead them to pray and* **ask God for His.**

This changes the interaction from horizontal (looking to you for advice) to vertical (looking to God for guidance).

Normally how God leads me to do this with friends or those I mentor is

1. **Listen** to them.
2. **Before giving advice** or even Bible verses, **say, "Let's pray and ask God what He wants to do about that."**
3. **Encourage them to ask God themselves,** *"Lord, what do You want to do?"* and give them time to listen. He might encourage them to forgive, or give them peace that He'll work things out. Or He might give them instructions.
4. **After they've shared what God is saying to their hearts, encourage them** with Scripture, personal experiences,

advice or whatever else you feel backs up what He's saying. You can also teach them to use the Three-Fold Sieve to make sure God's the One leading them in that direction.

If they don't feel God showing them anything during that time of prayer, barriers like doubt, pride or fear might be in the way. Or sometimes they already know what God wants them to do, but they're hoping He'll change His answer.

You can continue in prayer together, asking God what those barriers are or urge them to leave their heart open before the Lord, listening for His answer in the days ahead.

Then, if the Spirit leads, you can share what you felt God showing you and any related Bible verses.

But whatever you say will not be complete without them hearing directly from the Lord. **They need a personal encounter with Jesus** for His truth to move from head knowledge to heart knowledge so they can walk out in it.

Another idea to help others tune their ears in to the Lord is to study the Bible together, but rather than you teaching or preaching on a passage, *let the Lord be the Teacher*.

You can do this method one-on-one with a friend, or together with a group of friends:

1. Before you read a passage, **urge them to ask God personally to speak to them through His Word.** This changes the relationship from horizontal ("I wonder what he's going to teach on today.") to vertical ("I wonder what *God* will say to me.")

2. Then **read it out loud.** I like to ask them to close their Bibles and their eyes and listen for the words, phrases or pictures that jump out at them.

3. **Ask them to share with the group what God was saying.**

This method is exciting, because each person faces different trials, and what God highlights for one person may be different from someone else. As they share their experiences with Him in that passage, they teach each other, and each person walks away feeling closer to the Lord because *He spoke to them personally and through them powerfully*.

You can do this with any passage God leads you to, but Psalm 23 is a fun one to start with. Try that with some friends or family members today. Write what God said to each person.

_____
_____
_____
_____

Another fun way to help others listen to God and follow His guidance is to read a passage (the stories from Jesus' life are especially fun) and ask those gathered to picture it as you read. Have them ask God which character they are most like in that scene, and to look for Jesus. What is He saying to them? What is He doing?

Try that right now yourself with Mark 2:1-12. Write what He shows you.

_____
_____
_____
_____

~ 35 ~

Get in the habit

of not just talking about prayer, but modeling it. When people come to you for advice or a decision needs to be made, don't just talk off the top of your head. Pray together. Asking God to speak into the situation, and listening to what HE has to say. Help others around you move from horizontal habits of asking for advice to vertical ones of listening to God.

36

DARE

to love

The greatest power on earth

Have you ever met Christians who look down on others because they don't do this or that or don't do it "right"? Explain.

_____

_____

_____

Like "cookie cutters," they want every Christian to look alike. But this life isn't about fitting into Joe Christian's box of dos and don'ts. What happens to people like that? See Isaiah 28:10-13.

_____

_____

_____

_____

Scary, isn't it? I'd rather walk in the freedom God gives me to be all He has made me to be, in my own uniqueness of loving Him and looking like Him, not Joe!

"Love the Lord your God with all your heart, with all your soul, and with all your mind. This is the first and great commandment. And the second is like it: 'You shall love your neighbor as yourself.' On these two commandments hang all the Law and the Prophets." Matthew 22:37-40

So, reduced to one word, what is the only thing we're to be about? __ __ __ __

The two commands of that Matthew passage knock down every brick of the prison walls of legalism, because it's not about how well you perform at this or that, but…

Did you love? Did you love God? Did you love others? _Then you have obeyed._

In tenth grade, one of my best friends was not a Christian. She loved to argue all her rea-

sons why she shouldn't believe in God. Sometimes I just listened; sometimes I spoke truth. But I don't remember feeling defensive. I just loved her and longed for her to know Jesus.

When another girl in our class said mean things about me, I said nice things back.

"Why do you do that?" asked my loyal lost friend, who respected me for my faith but couldn't understand it. I told her again of God's love. Romans 12:9-21.

For many years, she remained one of my closest friends ever. But it wasn't until she had children of her own that she had a change of heart toward Christ.

Her unbelieving home had been one of strife, but my Christian home had been one of love. She wanted her children to grow up with love like that and she knew from our conversations that _Jesus was the reason for that love._

So one morning, she told God that if He was real, she would follow Him, but He would have to tell her how. Thousands of miles away, I felt the Lord prompting me to call her. And moments later, my friend I had loved for 25 years came to Jesus.

Now she has grown so fast in the Lord that she is one of my favorite people in this world to talk with about the deeper things of God.

Love changes lives.

Unfortunately, people have a tendency to create love boxes—ideas of what they think love is—and then try to fit themselves or others into them.

But if we love as God loves, we love without boundaries. We love, not because the person deserves it, but _because He first loved us._ 1 John 4:19-21. _We forgive,_ not because what they did was okay, but _because we have been_

forgiven. Matthew 6:14-15.

Likewise, because boundless Kingdom Love doesn't fit in human boxes, it may look different in each situation. The same Jesus who spoke gently and extended grace to an adulteress called the religious leaders "vipers." John 8:3-11, Matthew 23:33.

One seems more loving than the other by human definition, but God knows each man's heart. A rebuke may be just what Love orders at times. 2 Timothy 4:2.

Love is surprising.

In one situation, God may ask you to love by helping someone. In another, He might ask you to let him do it himself. Each person, situation and relationship is so unique, and God's love is so wide and deep and long and high (Ephesians 3:14-19), that the realm of possibilities of what He might ask you to do out of love should not be limited to your understanding and expectations, but handed over to the One Whose name is Love.

Love is forever.

God's love is everlasting and inclusive. So as best you can, live at peace with others. Ephesians 4:1-6. Let them know you're willing to work things out, no matter how long it takes or how painful the process, and that you love them and accept them, even if their ideas are different than yours.

Love accepts.

God is holy and perfect, and yet He accepts us and loves us just as we are at each stage along our journey, mistakes and all.

Love so deeply that others do not fear you as someone who angers easily and seeks ret-

ribution. 1 John 4:18. Rather, be the one who fights for them and speaks God's words of love and truth to help them through.

Love overcomes.

When I was single, rather than ask God for a long list of traits I wanted in a husband, I prayed that he would love God first and love me second. I knew that if I married a man of love (which is one of God's names, 1 John 4:16), we could make it through anything together. *And we have.*

How can you show God your love today?

_____

_____

Prayerfully read John 13:34-35, 15:12; Romans 12:9-18; and 1 Corinthians 13. Write down some things love does.

_____

_____

_____

_____

And some things love does *not* do.

_____

_____

_____

In what ways have you been unloving?

_____

_____

_____

How do you feel God leading you to show love to others today? This week? How is that a demonstration of His love?

_____

_____

_____

36

Get in the Habit

of asking God how to love those around you the way He loves them. Be willing to love even the unlovely. Let your love be freely given, not expecting anything in return, even as God has freely given you His love.

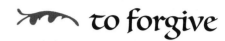 to forgive

Forgiveness is a choice

Imagine a kite flying high and free upon the wind, no strings attached. ... Now imagine that kite's string *tied to the bars of a prison cell.*

Your heart was created to fly high and free in the joy and peace that come from knowing without a doubt the unending depths and heights of God's love.

But most people don't walk in that kind of freedom. Bound to lies that push them to fear, anger and self-protection (John 8:42-47), they lash out at others, doing and saying hurtful things. *If you don't forgive them, it's like tying your heartstrings to their prison cell, letting their junk jerk you around.*

You think about what they did to you, imagine what you'll say next time you see them, plot ways to avoid them, think up how to get back at them. Their offense plays over again in your mind, controlling your thoughts. **You need to cut the string and be free!**

What does Matthew 6:14-15 say happens to those who don't forgive? _____

_____

What does Ephesians 4:26-27 say happens if you let the sun go down on your anger?

_____

_____

Did you know **most cases of depression and suicide can be traced back to unforgiveness?** If you don't forgive straight away, even for a terrible offense that doesn't "deserve" forgiveness, your anger can ferment into bitterness, feeding depression and suicide.

Unforgiveness is seriously dangerous business! Don't wait for that person to ask forgiveness. *Just forgive.*

Confronting someone on a sin is certainly

in line (Matthew 18:15), especially when you do it in love. But most offenders are too blinded by strongholds like pride and self-defense to apologize or acknowledge wrongdoing.

You are the one who suffers when you don't forgive, not your offender.

Before we go further, it's important that you know what forgiveness is not.

- **Forgiveness is not saying what that person did was okay**. Sin is never okay.

- **Forgiveness is not forgetting the event**, although forgetting might happen once you forgive.

- **Forgiveness is not letting a person do the same ugly things to you over and over** and just "taking" it.

Forgiveness is releasing that person into the hands of God for Him to deal with, and releasing your own heart from the chains that bind you to the sin done against you.

God is your Vindicator. Isaiah 50:6-11. *He* is the One who judges each person's actions and deals with them accordingly, not you.

Steps to freedom through forgiveness:

1. **Before you judge the other person for what he did wrong, make sure the sin isn't actually your own.**

Did you do something to instigate the other person's response? Are you also in some way guilty of what you're accusing him of? Are you judging or mind-reading (deciding what he's thinking or what motive he had)? Matthew 7:1-5, James 4:10-12.

The best way to miss what God's doing in you is to point your finger at someone else.

In fact, *you're likely to find yourself in the*

same situations over and over until you finally address the mess inside you and change.

Most of our pain comes from our own wrong thought processes. So,

2. **Whenever you feel angry or hurt, go to your divine Counselor and ask Him why you feel that way.** Ask Him when was the first time that feeling or response developed in your life, and let Him take you anywhere He wants to take you and show you anything He wants to show you. He may bring back a childhood memory.

3. **Allow yourself to remember that event and feel what you felt when it happened.** Look for the lies (like, "Everyone's against me. I have to defend myself.")

4. **Still in that memory, choose to forgive.**

   - **Say, "*I forgive (name) for (offense)."***
   - **Lay down all your opinions and ideas about that person at Jesus' feet and ask for His.**
   - **Pray for him and bless him.**

5. **If you made a vow** (like, "I'll never let anyone do that to me again!") **break it.** (See Chapter 23.)

6. **Ask God for His truth.** "Lord, You were there when that happened. What were You doing and saying?" Run it through the Three-Fold Sieve (Chapter 13).

7. **Now forgive the offender in your current situation. Bless him. Pray for him.**

8. **If the offense replays in your mind,** don't worry about it, no matter how many times it happens, just **remind yourself, "I forgive ... and I bless him in Jesus' name,"** and then pray for him again. If

you pray all the more for others' salvation and freedom when Satan attacks you, eventually he'll leave you alone and that old offense won't come to mind anymore.

Forgiveness is a decision. Even if you don't "feel" forgiving, make a conscious choice to forgive and your heart will eventually follow.

When our son was in middle school, one boy rallied others to beat on him for no apparent reason. Even as they pummeled him, he forgave them. One of the boys was so touched by his grace he asked forgiveness.

But not the one who instigated the fight. Our son sought ways to love him, be a friend to him and include him when others did not. He even forgot about the incident. Eventually, through his love, **that boy came to Christ.**

"If we walk in the light as He is in the light, we have fellowship with one another." 1 John 1:7a

Ask God, "Is there anyone I haven't forgiven?" Look for sin and wrong thought processes. Are you judging? Acting vindictively?

Follow the steps in this chapter to forgive and write your experience here.

Don't let others' junk jerk you around. Be the bigger man. *Forgive.*

⤙ 37 ⤚

Get in the Habit
of immediately forgiving anyone who offends you. After all, you too have said or done hurtful things before, and God and others have forgiven you. So be willing to forgive quickly, even if others don't ask for forgiveness. Maybe, just maybe, your forgiveness will change them.

to see with God's eyes

Don't judge by appearances

What did Jesus say in John 7:24? _____

_____

_____

🐦 *Beware of first impressions.*

Who did Samuel think should be king? See 1 Samuel 16:1-13. Why?

_____

_____

_____

Who was the one God chose instead?

_____

Man looks at the _____ ; God looks at the _____ . (v 7)

In all things, don't lean on your own understanding** (Proverbs 3:5-6; 1 Corinthians 8:1), **but ask God what He sees and join Him in His viewpoint.

Not long ago, a cluster of villages that had never heard the Gospel was on our hearts. A bit off the beaten track, the trip would require an overnight stay, but we didn't know anyone yet who lived there.

On our way to a different area, we stopped to eat lunch. As we prayed for God to lead us, a vivacious teenager bounced into the restaurant and sat down at our table, chattering all about herself. We didn't know her, so her behavior was odd and the interruption annoying. Everything inside me wanted to brush her off. ... Everything, that is, but *Jesus.*

He reminded me to not judge by appearances, but to look for what He was doing. So I listened more carefully to her prattle.

Not only was she hungry for the Lord, but she was from the area God had laid on my heart! That very next week, she took us to her village. They heard the Gospel for the first time ever, and that girl came to Christ.

🐦 *Beware of assumptions.*

Can you think of a time when you said one thing, but someone else understood something else? How did that make you feel?

_____

_____

You can try your best to speak honestly and clearly so others will understand your heart and motives. But you can't control what they will think. ***People believe whatever they want to, regardless of whether it's true or not.***

But *don't be like the world.* Our enemy wants to divide and destroy. He would love to make up quite a story in your head to turn you against your brother or sister. So, **don't assume you know what someone is thinking**. *Ask, "When you said ..., did you mean ...?"*

There is only one Judge. James 4:11-12. And He didn't die and give you His job. So **don't assess a situation based on what you think you discern or even your own experience.** *Ask God how He sees it.*

Spend time in God's presence, surrendering your thoughts and opinions over to Him, so you can take on the mind of Christ.

When someone in authority told us we had to move to a smaller apartment, rather than give in to bitterness or complaining, we asked God for His viewpoint.

He said, "I have a castle prepared for you." We laughed, thinking we must have heard Him wrong. But our hearts were at peace. We knew whatever His plans, they were good.

When the time came to move two years later, the perfect apartment opened up, and the lock on the door was *in the shape of a castle!*

We laughed so hard. But then, as an act of worship, we decorated our new apartment to remind us of the castle Jesus is preparing for us in heaven. John 14:1-3. What could have been a time of bitterness became a joy as we stepped into what God was showing us.

But often, if I don't ask Him what He's doing, He may not show me, and then I could miss the miracle.

🙠 *Beware of that pretty face.*

It's easy to believe you are in love with a beautiful girl because of the rush you feel when you're around her. But that feeling may not be from God, even if she's a Christian.

As we saw in Chapter 27, Step 9, demonic forces may be at work to draw you in and block you from God's purposes.

You could end up settling for less than the best, and even a mess, simply because *your heart yelled at you over the Spirit's whispered warning.* Proverbs 5.

So be on the alert in matters of the heart, because *your own heart may not be something you can trust.* Jeremiah 17:9.

If the woman you're attracted to is indeed the "one," your callings and focus on God will align, not just the rush in your body. (See Chapter 39.)

🙠 *Come up here.*

A few years ago, a close friend made some wrong judgments about me and cut off our friendship, unwilling to hear the truth or work it out. As I took my pain to God, His heart said to mine, "Come up here."

He showed me how He too had been misjudged and betrayed by those He loved, and how joining in His suffering made me one with Him. Romans 8:17, Philippians 3:7-11.

Those times when I let go of my opinions and let God give me His Eagle-eye perspective, I now call "Come-up-here" moments.

When my feet are planted in mud and my problems are up in my face, I miss the bigger picture. But *when He lifts me up to see what He's doing through it all, suddenly my problems seem small in the light of His majesty.*

Often, He shows me what He's doing in others or in me; or even globally. But **His viewpoint radically changes my heart and heals me.**

What situations or people are you struggling with at this moment? Spend time in worship, laying your opinions and ideas of that person or circumstance at Jesus' feet and asking Him for His. Run what He says to you through the Sieve in Chapter 13, and write it here: _____

_____
_____
_____
_____
_____
_____

🙠 38 🙢

Get in the habit

of not judging by appearances. Don't decide that your opinions and ideas are right, or that others are wrong. Just lay your ideas about people and situations at Jesus' feet and look for what He says on the matter. His opinion is the only true one, and the only one that truly matters. God, His truth, His purposes and His kingdom are more REAL than anything temporary you can see or feel on this earth. As you look through His eyes, seeing what He sees, He will empower you to rise up on eagle's wings and soar over your problems in ways you could never do relying on your own experience or understanding.

to choose God's choice

Kingdom culture relating

As we said in the last chapter, *just because you are attracted to a girl doesn't mean she's the one God has for you to marry.*

So how will you find this Godly, perfect wife? What is your current dating strategy?

_____

_____

_____

In some cultures, a boy might ask out a girl he thinks is "hot" even if he doesn't know her. He might kiss her and more; then decide later whether or not he wants to ask her out again.

Nowhere in the Bible is this Kingdom Culture. Nor is homosexuality. Leviticus 18:22, 20:13, 1 Corinthians 6:9-11, Romans 1:26-28, 1 Timothy 1:10-11. And yet, that also has become accepted behavior in many cultures, even among some Christians.

One of the difficulties with dating is *our hearts get so emotionally caught up in the moment, together with attraction and lust, that we may not be able to distinguish the Spirit's leading in the midst of it all.* Jeremiah 17:9.

Have you ever experienced that? Have you ever been attracted to someone you realized later was not God's choice for you? Explain.

_____

_____

_____

That's why it's important to *know what you're looking for in a wife* before you ever go out on that first date.

Matthew 22:37-40 is always at the core of everything Kingdom Culture. So, let's use it as a gauge for dating practices:

Is it loving God to use His temple (your body) for sin? To bow to lust and pride rather than to His Holiness? To let your own selfish desires guide you rather than His Holy Spirit?

Is it loving to your wife-to-be for you to look lustfully at another woman and fondle her? Is it loving to a daughter of the King to lead her into sin? To play around with her heart and body? To date her a couple of times and then reject her while you look for someone more appealing? Is it loving to her husband-to-be for you to kiss his wife?

Emphatically not. Read 1 Thessalonians 4:3-8, Colossians 3:5, 2 Timothy 2:22, 1 Timothy 4:12, Ephesians 5:1-3, 1 Corinthians 6:12-20, Galatians 5:16-25, Romans 6:15-19 and 2 Corinthians 6:14. Add those together with 1 Timothy 5:1-2 and Matthew 22:37-40. What does God say about dating?

_____

_____

_____

As a man of God, **you are looking for a woman who loves God with all her heart.**

To find her, you must spend the time it takes to truly get to know her. But don't jump straight into a date to do that. You need to **be a brother to her first.** 1 Timothy 5:1-2. You don't go around kissing your sister, do you?

As you get to know this woman of God He might have for you, here are some questions for you to consider:

1. Do you enjoy being with her? Why? Do you have things in common?

2. Are you hiding anything from her? Why?

3. Does she get offended easily?

4. Does she gossip?

5. What does she spend her money on? Does she save? Does she work hard?

6. Is she trustworthy? Does she do what she says? Keep her word?

7. Does she willingly help her family with chores or does she complain?

8. Is she studying the Word? Does she talk about what God's teaching her?

9. Does she seek out opportunities to serve God and others?

10. Watch how she acts around her family and friends. Is she kind? Does she treat her parents with respect?

11. Does she pray? How do you know?

12. Is she just talking about God or have you actually watched her live a life of surrender and obedience?

As you get to know her, ask her what God is teaching her in her quiet times and how that is affecting her life situations.

Get to know her passions. What is God calling her to do with her life? That's important, because if God is calling you into the ministry or to be a missionary in a foreign country, but she doesn't want that kind of life, then *she might not be the one He has for you.*

Are there any other qualities you'd like to have in a wife? Ask God for that.

Now, look back at all those qualities and questions. If she were to run *you* through that same test, how would you fare?

Finding the woman of God He desires for you to marry begins first with *you being the man of God she desires to marry.*

As you seek God's will and grow in friendship together, if you and she both feel a peace that God could be bringing you together for marriage, *then* it's time to think about dating.

Pray together, read the Word together, worship together, talk together, grow together in Him. **Let your relationship be founded on God, not fleshly desires.**

Are you in a dating relationship now? Or contemplating one? Lay that down before the Lord. If you feel it's not what God has for you, seek Him for the most loving way to end it. Do you need to ask her forgiveness? To pray for her and bless her and the man she'll marry? Ask God, and then follow His lead.

If you have been in an intimate sexual relationship outside of marriage, you have bound yourself "as one" with that person. 1 Corinthians 6:12-20, Matthew 5:27-28. If you haven't done Step 7 yet in Chapter 27, take time now to repent and cut off those unholy ties:

"Lord forgive me for (sin). In the name of Jesus, I break any unholy ties to (name), and I bless her and her future marriage to be founded on You, for You alone are True Love. Set me free from the thought processes that lead me in wrong directions, and set me apart for the one You have chosen for me to marry. Teach me how to remain pure and led by Your Spirit in my choices. Help me to be the man of God you want me to be as a husband and lead me to Your choice in Your perfect timing...."

⚜ 39 ⚜

Get in the habit

of not thinking below the belt. Don't let fantasies and attractions lead you, but seek the Lord. Be clear on what woman-of-God qualities you are seeking in a wife, and don't settle for anything less than God's best. Seek to become the man of God she will want to marry.

to submit to authority

Blessing those over you

I once had a Christian boss who dictated what I could and could not wear. He paid women less than men; and promoted his unqualified friends over me, even though I had experience and tenure.

Often he fabricated stories in his head about me, and then barged into my office to angrily accuse. If I smiled and listened, he fumed all more, "Why aren't you crying?"

When he found out God was calling us overseas, he terminated my job early and cheated me out of more than $1000.

Was it easy submitting to that man? No. In fact, to keep my heart in the right place, I had to write on a card in bold letters, "I don't work for (that man); I work for God," and tape it where I saw it every day. God gave me the grace and wisdom I needed in each circumstance, and I not only made it through, I grew.

Not all bosses are like that. But the truth is you may find it easier to submit to God than to the human He places over you.

You please God just by being His son, after all. But some earthly authorities are impossible to please.

What if your boss, teacher, or parent is irrational, demanding, controlling or vindictive? What if he asks you to do things you can't? Or even something immoral?

How does God want us to act toward our leaders? See Titus 3:1-2. _____
_____
_____

Why? See Hebrews 13:17.
_____
_____
_____

What is to be our attitude toward governing authorities and police? 1 Peter 2:13-17. Why?
_____
_____
_____

How does 1 Thessalonians 5:12-13 say we should treat those in authority over us?
_____
_____
_____

That's a lot of verses on submitting to authority, isn't it? And we haven't even scratched the surface yet.

God is perfect and holy, and yet He places imperfect people in leadership positions over us and then asks us to obey them. Why?

To testify of His greatness. Daniel 1:17-21.

In the story of Joseph, each time he was wronged and his position was knocked down to the worst degree, he worked for those above him as unto the Lord. God blessed him, he gained favor, and God used him for His glory.

What about Daniel and his friends? In what ways did they glorify God under the pagan king who captured them and dragged them from their homeland? See Daniel 1:17-21.
_____
_____
_____

Daniel excelled in his work and was given a chance to testify to the king about God. How did the king respond? See Daniel 2.
_____
_____
_____

To grow. 2 Corinthians 12:7-10.

Each time my boss did something unjust or

made my job more difficult, I had a choice: to be angry and bitter, or to join God in what He was doing. When I chose the latter, my heart was free and I grew stronger in the Lord.

But I grow much faster under good leaders. The editor at my first writing job marked up my news articles with myriads of red scribbles. But I would never be the writer I am today without his encouragement and correction.

And when I began doing women's ministry, my leader modeled a lifestyle of worship and surrender. When I did something that hurt others, she confronted me and helped me become more loving.

One friend had a boss once who didn't support him. So when he joined a new team, he did things behind his new leader's back, rallying others to join him. At last, he realized this leader truly loved him and was *for* him. He asked forgiveness, and received the blessing of a Godly covering under a man who helped him grow in character and faith.

Submit to your leaders, be a joy not a burden, pray for them, respect them, love them, live in peace with them, and honor them.

Whatever you do, do it as unto the Lord.
1 Corinthians 10:31-33, Ephesians 6:5-8.

Remember He will strengthen you. Philippians 4:13. So no matter what job you do, keep your conversation running with Him. Let Him guide you through each difficulty, flood you with His peace (Philippians 4:5-7), and make even the hard things turn out for good. Romans 8:28.

But what if your leader forbids you from doing something God has asked you to do? What did Shadrach, Meshach, and Abednego do? See Daniel 3.

Sometimes standing up for the things of the Lord can be costly. We have friends who served God as leaders in a Christian organization for nearly 20 years, but when edicts came down from above which were contrary to the Word but which they were required to enforce, they resigned. All those years down the drain? No. They obeyed the Lord, and obeying God is never a waste! Deuteronomy 28:13.

My husband and I work in a country where Christians are often arrested and beaten for their faith. We know at any moment we could be ripped from our home as Daniel was in Daniel 6. But will we stop worshipping God and living for Him, sharing His love with others? Not likely!

So if a day comes that you, like Daniel, must stand up and say to someone in authority over you, "I will not bow to your idols," then do so with love, bringing glory to God.

What authority figures are in your life right now (parents, teachers, employers, government leaders, etc.)? Pray for them and ask God to show you specific ways you can bless them. Write what God shows you, and then step out in obedience.

Get in the Habit

of submitting to your leaders and being a blessing to them. If you honor those in authority over you and do all your work as unto the Lord, He will bless you, just as He did Joseph.

41 Chapter

DARE

to walk in integrity

Living from the inside out

Are you the same person when others are watching as you are when no one else is around?

Seeking to understand the road laws in the country where we live, we asked our taxi driver, "Can you turn right on red here?"

"Sometimes," he answered.

"What does that mean, 'sometimes?'"

"Well, if a policeman's there, you can't. But if he's not, you can."

Funny huh? ... But what do *you* think?

It's past midnight, no cars are coming. Do you run that red light? Do you slide through that stop sign?

Do you watch that movie when no one knows you are? Go to certain sites on your computer? Masturbate?

That's a tough one. After all, who's to know? You're not hurting anyone when there's no one around to be hurt, right?

Integrity begins on the inside.

What does Ephesians 5:1-18 say about hiding sin? What does God's light do to it?

What are you to be filled with that is so different from the rest of the world? (v 18)

What does Luke 11:33-36 say to your heart?

In light of that Scripture, how might watching a sex scene in a movie affect your relationship with Christ and your testimony to others, even if no one knows you watched it?

What you do in the dark is not hidden from the spiritual realm.

The truth is *whatever you hide in secret the enemy can use against you.* So, if you are entangled in a secret sin or in thoughts that lead you there, it's a good idea to share with someone you trust who will pray with you and help you to freedom before it gets worse.

Okay, now that we've established that a man of God lives from the inside out (that inside being filled with the Holy Spirit), let's look on the outside.

Integrity speaks of a man's reputation, especially his honesty and high moral values.

For example, a man of integrity

- Doesn't lie. Colossians 3:9.
- Seeks out the truth and speaks it boldly.
- Keeps his promises.
- Doesn't steal, cheat, or engage in thoughts or deeds of darkness in secret. Ephesians 5:11-21.
- Doesn't slander, but speaks good things behind others' backs. Romans 12:9-21.
- Is a man others feel they can trust or confide in.
- Is known for his love for God.
- Has the reputation of not just reading God's Word but living it. James 1:22, Galatians 2:20.
- Fears God, rather than man. Galatians 1:10.

A man of integrity doesn't let the persuasive words of others move him to do something contrary to his convictions, but he unwaveringly stands on the Word with Christ as his model. Ephesians 5:1, 1 John 4:19.

"'Teacher,' they said, 'we know you are a man of integrity and that you teach the way of God in accordance with the truth. You aren't swayed by men, because you pay no attention to who they are.'" Matthew 22:16b (NIV)

My husband is a man of integrity. Many times, I have watched him stand his ground to do what God and the Word tell him to, even in the face of opposition.

One time, some friends tried to get us to break a law. They had "good" reasons, but our two children watching us was reason enough not to. 1 Peter 2:13-17.

"Encourage the young men to be self-controlled. In everything set them an example by doing what is good. In your teaching show integrity, seriousness, and soundness of speech that cannot be condemned, so that those who oppose you may be ashamed because they have nothing bad to say about us." Titus 2:6-8 (NIV)

I feel so honored to be married to a man who lets the Word guide his actions, rather than the persuasive arguments of men. Romans 13:1-3.

Men of integrity often have the best marriages, are the best fathers, get the best jobs, find the most fulfillment in life. But ...

The greatest reward you will enjoy as a man of integrity is God's presence.
Exodus 33:11-17.

"I know that You are pleased with me, for my enemy does not triumph over me. **In my integrity, You uphold me and set me in Your presence forever.**" Psalm 41:11-12 (NIV)

The Word is full of instructions on how to live a life of integrity before God and man. Each one is a jewel that brings freedom and purpose to your life. Psalm 119:17-22.

Check out the following verses and write what these men of integrity were characterized by:

Proverbs 10:9: _____
Proverbs 11:3: _____
Proverbs 13:6: _____
Psalm 25:21: _____
Psalm 78:70-72: _____
1 Kings 9:1-5: _____
Nehemiah 7:2: _____
Psalm 7: _____

Pray and ask God to show you any "secrets" that are making you stumble. Write a prayer of release from these, cutting off the enemy's rights to attack you in those areas, and surrendering your thoughts to God. You can use 2 Corinthians 10:3-5 as a model, if you like.

_____
_____
_____
_____
_____
_____
_____
_____
_____
_____
_____
_____
_____
_____

～ 41 ～

Get in the habit

of baring your heart before God. He already knows all your secrets, so it doesn't do you any good to "hide" anything from Him. Instead, let Him show you how to let go of the things that mar you, so you can grab hold of the things that build you. You want to be known as someone others can trust, a faithful friend and husband, who does the right thing out of love for both God and those around you. 1 Peter 4:15-19.

to glorify God in everything

The highest honor

In ninth grade, a burly Korean boy threw a fastball, and the first baseman ducked. That's what you do when Big Kim throws the ball: you get out of the way. But I missed that advice somehow, and caught it in my face!

As I sprawled out on the grass, the top half of my vision in blackness, my friend DJ's face appeared in the bottom half, just beyond a tuft of grass, grinning in fascination. "Look! Her nose is on the other side of her face!" (DJ is now a doctor, by the way.)

Kim felt so bad about what happened that he came to my house nearly every day to check on me. My face was a purple mess, I could barely see and I had difficulty breathing, so I wasn't up to visitors. But I sent him messages through my father. I wanted Kim to know I forgave him and Jesus loves him.

Repeatedly, Kim asked, "How can she forgive me after what I've done?" Repeatedly, my father shared with him about God's love and the difference He makes in our lives.

After a couple of weeks and some creative plastic surgery to put my nose back where it belonged, Kim showed back up at my house, this time with a tiny gold cross he had brought as a gift. Tears in his eyes, he said, "I decided to follow Jesus, and I wanted you to be the first to know."

I still have that gold cross today. It's a mark of God's glory I will never forget.

You know, come to think of it, my Jesus got beat up, too, so that I might be saved. I wonder if I looked a bit like Him during those black-and-blue days. Matthew 27:30.

Hopefully, you won't ever get your nose or anything else busted up, but spiritually speaking, the more you look like Jesus, the more glory you bring Him. Philippians 3:7-11. *His glory is what you were created for.* Isaiah 43:7.

He has set you on a pilgrimage to know Him ever deeper, and to make Him known ever louder, as He transforms you into His likeness with ever-increasing glory.
2 Corinthians 3:12-18.

The more you love—love God and love others—the more you will look like Him and bring Him glory. Matthew 22:37-40.

Let the things you do every day be the things that turn eyes God's way.

You'll make mistakes sometimes. Everyone does. But even your sins and flaws can point people to the Lord. In fact, saying, "I was wrong; please forgive me" to someone you've hurt *SPARKLES* with His glory. 1 John 1.

So don't be afraid of your mistakes. Make them an opportunity to bless others.

Yes, bless! People don't like it when you pretend you're perfect. They'd rather see you real: sharing your troubles with them, admitting when you're wrong, serving the Lord because it comes from your heart, not just to put on a show.

It's possible that one day people will know of you because of something you've done in this life, but my prayer is that it will be something *He* has done, not you, and that no one will be able to mistake that. Psalm 115:1.

Do only the things God asks of you.

Once you prove yourself a faithful follower of Christ, many people may ask you to do this or that. They might even use guilt or manipulation. But worrying about what others expect of you can lead to burnout.

Burnout happens when you do more than God asks, or you do it in your own power.

So, please don't go there! You're too important a star to burn out. Daniel 12:3.

Even if people get angry, do only what God asks you to, and then lean on His strength to do it, not your own. Colossians 1:28-29, 2 Corinthians 12:9-10, Philippians 4:13.

✒ *Leave plenty of time in your schedule to be alone with the Lord.*

One of my mentors used to say, "If on any given day, there's no room in your schedule to spend 1-4 hours with the Lord, then there's something wrong with your schedule."

She has a point. If you don't spend time with God, how will you know Him? *It's like marrying a wife, and then ignoring her.*

You might even want to schedule personal retreats with the Lord in addition to your quiet times, where you can steal away with Him for a whole day, or even several days.

Remember, you were made for relationship. **If you make glorifying God about what you do, rather than about being one with Him, you'll miss the whole point.**

✒ *Make the most of every opportunity.*
Ephesians 5:18.

I hopped in a taxi one day for a ten-minute ride to the bus station in the closed country where we live. Within seconds, the driver began confessing his sin of adultery to me. I didn't know the language well at that time, so in my "baby talk," I asked, "Would you like to wash your heart?"

"Yes!" he cried. "How can I?"

I told him God loves him and sent His Son to die for him so his sins could be forgiven and he could have eternal life. Right there, in five minutes of hearing about God's love, that man gave his heart to Christ.

I handed him a Bible in his language that I just happened to have in my bag (God had planned this encounter from the start!), and as I hurried off to catch my bus, he yelled after me, clutching his new treasure to his chest, "I can't wait to tell my wife!"

A lot can happen in ten minutes.

"Therefore, my beloved brethren, be steadfast, immovable, always abounding in the work of the Lord, knowing that your labor is not in vain in the Lord." 1 Corinthians 15:58

What opportunities to give God glory are in your path right now? Are there things you're doing He didn't ask you to do? Or things you're doing in your own strength rather than surrendering to His empowering?

_____
_____
_____
_____
_____

Hand every opportunity over to God to make sure He's asking you to do it. Then seek Him to do it through you, for you, and even, perhaps, despite you. 2 Corinthians 12:9-10.

Write John 3:30 into a prayer. _____
_____
_____
_____
_____
_____

✒ 42 ✒

Get in the Habit

of seeking to bring glory to God every moment of every day. Stay close to Him, asking Him what He's doing and listening for His answers, so you walk in step with Him. Galatians 5:25. And shine! every moment, every day. Let Him be your Light, as you light the way to Him for others. Daniel 12:3.

"The things that you have heard from me among many witnesses, commit these to faithful men who will be able to teach others also."

2 Timothy 2:2

Leader's Guide

to lead a group study

Deepen the dare

Is God leading you to study this workbook together with other young men? Are you a parent who would like to study these chapters together with your son(s)?

"Where two or three are gathered together in My name, I am there in the midst of them."
Matthew 18:20

Studying the Word together with others is powerful, not only because of the above verse, but also because, as the body of Christ, we are each unique in our giftings and experiences with Him. We need each other in order to gain "the whole measure" of the fullness of Christ." Ephesians 4:1-16.

So, before I share with you some suggestions, let me pray for you.

"Father, thank You for Your servant who has chosen to make a difference in the lives of these young men. Pour out Your anointing and Your blessing, and unleash Your power to flow in mighty measures as they gather to meet with You. Open the doors of each heart, and then rage in like a mighty flood. Invade their space, get up in their face, and speak so loudly that none can deny You are near. On Your servant who is leading, I ask for an extra measure of wisdom, sensitivity to Your leading, surrender to You, and empowering to walk out in this challenge each week. When we feel weak, Lord, make us strong. May our teaching not be with persuasive words, but with Your power, so that all eyes are turned to You." 1 Corinthians 2:4-5, 13; Deuteronomy 32:2; 2 Corinthians 12:9-10; Colossians 1:28-29.

Here are some suggestions for leading a group in studying this book:

1. The smaller the group, the safer some will feel to share and the easier it will be for everyone to participate. Generally, groups of 4-8 make for the best discussions. But ask the Lord what He wants to do.

2. As young men sign up, advise them to bring their Bibles, this book and a journal to the meetings (I have prepared a special journal for them you can find at MoreThanAConquerorBooks.com, if they would like to use that one). Encourage them to write in their journals every day, noting what God is teaching them in their quiet times and through life experiences. Make sure you keep one, too.

3. Note that some of the questions asked in this book are highly personal. If your group is tightly knit, they may want to be accountable to each other and pray for each other through those issues. But others may not, so let God lead you as you lead discussions.

4. Because the tools in this workbook for walking as one with Christ require practice in order to see transformation, you may only want to assign 1-2 chapters a week. Stay ahead, doing the studies yourself so you can gauge which weeks need more time, and so you can share your own experiences with God.

5. If the young men aren't doing the studies in their quiet times, just walk through the chapters in class instead, reading the scriptures and answering the questions together. For the more personal questions, just give them some time of silence to answer.

Be accountable.

If you don't already have a **mentor** (See

Chapter 34), pray and ask God about who will cover you in prayer. This could be a pastor, church staff member, or just a Godly friend.

You might also ask God to lead you to a **right-hand man** (one of the young men in your study or another man you trust) to come early and pray with you in the room, join in the meeting and then debrief with you afterward. If you can't lead one week for some reason, this person can step in for you.

➤ *Enlist intercessors.*

Get parents and other intercessors involved in praying for you and these young men as you study and meet each week. But keep private things said in your meetings confidential.

➤ *Stay ahead.*

Do these lessons in your quiet times, but don't wait until the day before you lead. Study them at least a week ahead so you have time to walk out in the truth and practical applications yourself before you teach them. The richness of your own experience will motivate others.

➤ *Pray.*

Follow the guideline in Chapter 32. The more you pray and surrender these studies and these young men into God's hands, the more powerfully He will move.

➤ *Begin with worship.*

I suggest about 20-30 minutes, as the Spirit leads, at the beginning of each meeting. This invites God's presence and helps everyone tune in to His voice.

Don't let anyone judge another for the way he worships, but let everyone feel comfortable.

You might want to intersperse spontaneous Scripture reading or prayer throughout the music or invite people to express verbally how great God is or read a psalm—however the Spirit leads.

Afterward, you might want to ask what they felt God saying during the worship time, before you move into the lesson.

You can lead the worship yourself or ask someone else. It's great to have live worship with instruments, and some of the young men in your group may be willing to help in this. But digital music is also an excellent option.

Compile a list of the participants' favorite worship songs, the ones that really touch their hearts, that you can draw from to arrange worship from week to week.

Tips on arranging a worship set:

1. For 20-30 minutes, you're usually looking at about 5-6 songs.

2. Make sure you have the words available for each person present.

3. Organizer-types might begin with praise songs about how wonderful God is and follow with more intimate songs, such as about how much He loves us and we love Him. Or you can do it the other way around. But my favorite way to arrange a worship set is to pray, then listen to God. Whatever songs pop into my mind after dedicating that time to Him, I arrange together how I feel Him leading me to.

4. The best way to know how to lead others in worship is to worship in your own quiet times.

➤ *Expect God to show up.*

Let the Holy Spirit have full freedom to lead you in His directions. Most definitely plan for each session, but listen to God as you plan, and surrender the meetings over to His leadership. If He takes you in a certain direction and the material isn't covered that week, just cover it the next week.

➤ *Pray for each other.*

Whenever someone shares a need or mentions something he feels God leading him to do, stop everything, gather around him, pray for him, and encourage him, reading any Scripture appropriate to the situation. This teaches the young men to minister to each other.

Encourage them to call each other during the week to ask about each other and pray for each other.

Be transparent.

Be real with these young men, so they will feel free to be real with you. Share about mistakes you've made and how God grew you through them. If you don't understand something in the study and aren't sure how to walk out in it, feel free to say so, and ask the boys to pray for you during your time together that week. Then be prepared to share the next week how God answered or how you are still working on that.

You are also free to write MoreThanAConquerorBooks@gmail.com to dialogue with the author about questions.

Keep confidentiality.

Whatever is shared in each session should stay within the group so that each person feels safe. If Joe tells a story, no one can tell it outside the meeting, unless Joe gives his permission.

Another key to helping the young men feel safe is to have a closed-door policy. Only those who are committed to come are allowed to come. No newcomers once the group has been established. But this needs to be discussed and prayed about together as a group. If, after the doors are closed, someone wishes to join, you should ask God about it together, because that person may be sent there by Him. So be flexible according to His leading.

The Word is your source.

If someone asks a question, don't just answer it off the top of your head. Make it an adventure to dig into the Word for the answer. If someone asks, "Is it okay to smoke?" for example, don't just say "No" or "Yes." Look up Scriptures in a concordance that deal with our bodies or glorifying God, and assign the boys to prayerfully read those Scriptures during the week, asking the Lord to speak to them. Then come together the next week to discuss what God said. Or read the Scriptures there in the meeting together, praying and asking God to speak. (See

Chapter 35.) This teaches them to go to God for the answers to all of life's questions.

Encourage discussion.

As you prepare, ask God to give you some good questions to ask from the lesson, or scriptures for the young men to discuss.

Some people are more talkative than others, so listen to the Lord as to how to draw the quiet ones out and rein in the vocal ones. You want everyone to participate, as He's doing different things in different people, and we all need each other to grow together in Him. Ephesians 4.

Ideas for discussion questions:

- What was this chapter about? Summarize in your own words.

- What did you like about this chapter? Why?

- What did you not like? Why?

- What touched you the most?

- Is there anything God is asking you to do? A command to follow? A sin to confess?

- How do you plan to walk out in that?

- How are you doing with walking out in what we talked about last week?

Give them opportunities to lead.

The ones who lead are usually the ones who grow the most (That means you, too!), so ask God to direct you in assigning tasks to different ones in your group to lead in prayer or worship or some of the sessions.

Have them take turns, so each one has a chance to develop and grow in different areas of leadership.

If you finish this study and want to do another, I recommend,

Dare to Become a Kingdom Culture Leader.

Find it now at

www.MoreThanAConquerorBooks.com.

You can also follow me on Twitter, Facebook, Pinterest and Wordpress.

Deepen the Dare

with these inspirational devotionals, Bible studies and novels by
Mikaela Vincent. Find these books and more at

MoreThanAConquerorBooks.com

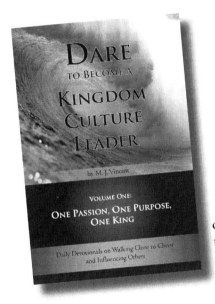

Dare to Become a Kingdom Culture Leader
Volume One: One Passion, One Purpose, One King
Volume Two: Oneness and the Watchman Warrior

Step into the destiny you were created for.
Become a Kingdom Culture Leader.

Most of us want to make a lasting difference here on earth. We
don't want to just live and die and be forgotten. Not that we need
to have some important name or
anything. But we want our lives
to count for something. Something that matters. Something

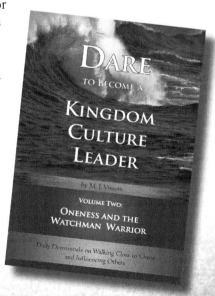

that lasts and influences others in such a way that this world is a
little brighter, a little better because we lived.

Whether you're a parent, teacher, pastor, missionary, leader,
or even just Joe Blow Christian, this book of daily devotions
and Bible studies is for you.

Through practical lessons on listening to God's voice, making wise decisions, following the Spirit's leading, walking in
humility, promoting unity, and leading others well, Vincent
digs into the Word to form new thought processes and habits
so we can keep in step with the King of Kings and lead out as
Kingdom Culture influencers.

Delight to Be a Woman of God

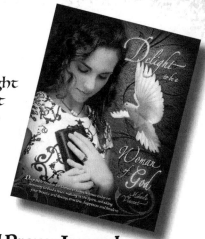

Do you have a sister or a friend who might benefit from deep Bible study too? *Delight to Be a Woman of God* is filled with Scripture and thought-provoking questions to teach young women to walk out in who they are as the bride of Christ, and to live and love through Christ's love. (Group study leader's guide included.)

Delight to Be a Woman of God Prayer Journal

Bible Studies and Devotionals for Middle School & Teens

Delight to Become a Woman of God

30 Bible studies from a mother's heart to her daughter's on drawing near to Christ and loving well

It's not a fairy tale. It's true. You really are a princess, destined to marry the King. And together you'll live happily forever after. It's all you ever dreamed life could be, and it's all yours, if you choose to become a woman of God. This Bible study guide for young women ages 12 and above, offers original illustrations, personal stories, deep questions, and Scripture to point young women to deeper depths with Christ so they can be set free from the things that keep them from the abundant life they were created for. A group study leader's guide is included. But this workbook can also be used for personal quiet times.

Dare to Become a Man of God

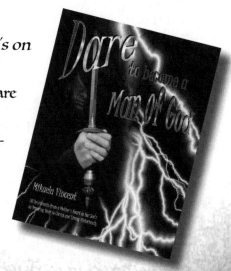

30 Bible studies from a mother's heart to her son's on drawing near to Christ and living victoriously.

Whether you like it or not, you are at war. Will you dare to defy enemy schemes? Will you dare to fight for the things that matter? Will you dare to become a man of God? Cartoons, personal stories, deep questions, practical how-to steps, and Scripture all point youth ages 12 and up to fix their eyes on Jesus and draw near to Him as they fight the good fight, listen to God's voice and make wise decisions through His guidance, so they can become more than conquerors through every tough situation life presents. A leader's guide is included, but this workbook can also be studied as a devotional in personal quiet times.

Christian Fantasy Adventure Novels with a Purpose

Rescue from Darkness
Book 1: Chronicles of the Kingdom of Light

Snatched from their summer fun by a sudden tragedy, six friends loyal to the King of Light embark upon an unforgettable adventure into the Kingdom of Darkness to rescue a young boy held hostage by evil creatures.

Astride such mystical mounts as a winged tiger, a flying unicorn, and a giant cobra, these ordinary young people engage in an extraordinary battle that will cost them more than they counted on.

As they struggle against monsters—and even each other—to overcome the fight against night, the friends soon discover the true enemy that must be conquered is the enemy within themselves.

Readers will enjoy a fun read while learning to listen to God's voice, walk in truth rather than lies, find freedom from fear, and fight the good fight.

Based on bedtime stories created by Vincent to help her children live who they are in Christ, this first book in the *Chronicles of the Kingdom of Light* is an inspirational allegory for young people filled with adventure, humor, and some truths that just might change their lives.

Sands of Surrender
Book 2: Chronicles of the Kingdom of Light

Banished by the King of Light, Cory cannot continue the search for his kidnapped brother until he discovers a way back into the Kingdom of Darkness where the boy is held prisoner. When creatures of Darkness offer to lead him there, he agrees to follow, a decision that costs him his freedom and exposes a plot against his family so dangerous he may not make it out alive.

Meanwhile, Victoria sets out on her own misadventure to rescue her friend, but her decisions place those she loves in such terrible peril, Cory's life is not the only one she must save.

Vincent uses humor and adventure to present truths that open the door to freedom from strongholds and generational curses, and walking in intimacy with the King of Kings.

Pure-As-Gold Children's Books

by Mikaela Vincent
MoreThanAConquerorBooks.com

*Equipping young hearts today
for the battles of tomorrow.*

Out You Go, Fear!

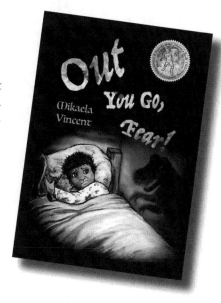

Is your child afraid of the night? Does he sometimes "see" monsters in the dark? Does she have nightmares or awake in a panic? Do you? This story about a fearful, but eventually brave boy addresses night fears most children experience. Through colorful pictures, sound truths, and a fun storyline, Vincent offers children ages 4-8 (and parents too!) steps to freedom from fear so they can sleep in peace. Includes tips for parents on helping their children to freedom from nightmares and the effects of traumatic memories.

I Want a Horse!

Have you ever wanted something so much it was all you could think of or dream about? In this inspirational picture book for ages 4-8, Mikaela Vincent uses colorful artwork, imaginative poetry and heartwarming humor to tell the story of a young girl who asks for her heart's desire only to discover a treasure she already has that surpasses her imaginations. Moms and daughters will especially enjoy a deep bond reading together this fun interchange between an ambitious little girl and her wise and creative mother.

I Want to See Jesus!

This easy-to-read book for ages 3-7 uses colorful drawings and simple words to teach just-beginning readers that Jesus is always with us, even when we can't see Him.

Made in the USA
Middletown, DE
11 September 2022